Guide to the
Superior Hiking Trail

Linking people with nature by footpath
along Lake Superior's North Shore

Guide to the
Superior Hiking Trail

Linking people with nature by footpath
along Lake Superior's North Shore

Edited by Andrew Slade
Ridgeline Press
2001

Guide to the Superior Hiking Trail

Printed in the United States of America
by McNaughton & Gunn, Inc.
First printing May 1993
Revised second printing November 1993
Revised third printing May 1995
Revised fourth printing April 1998
Revised fifth printing June 2001

Cover and text design: Sally Rauschenfels
Map illustrations: Matt Kania
Cover photo: Jay Steinke
Title page photo: Sam Cook
Illustrations: Dover

*Although the editors and publisher have researched all sources
to ensure the accuracy and completeness of the information
contained in this book, we assume no responsibility for errors,
inaccuracies, omissions or any inconsistency herein.*

ISBN: 0-9636598-2-0

Library of Congress Cataloging-in-Publication Data

Guide to the Superior Hiking Trail: linking people with nature by
    footpath along Lake Superior's North Shore.—Rev. fifth printing
        p.   cm.
    "Superior Hiking Trail Association"—T.p. verso.
    ISBN 0-9636598-2-0 (pbk.)
    1. Hiking—Minnesota—Superior Hiking Trail—Guidebooks.
    2. Superior Hiking Trail (Minn.)—Guidebooks. I. Superior Hiking Trail
Assocation.
GV199.42.M62S875   1998
917.76'7—dc21   98-16404
                                                              CIP

for Tom Peterson and Mark Wester,
the heart and soul of the Superior Hiking Trail

Acknowledgements

Many thanks to all who helped make this book happen.

Photography: Jay Steinke, cover photo and Sam Cook, title page photo.

Project Coordinator: Nancy Hylden (first edition), Nancy Odden (fourth and fifth editions).

Trail Correspondents: Bill Anderson, Jill Dalbacka, Ron Wolff, Bunter Knowles, Don Schlossnagle, Jim Erickson, Ann Russ, Andrew Slade, Ruth Hiland, Karen Hanson, Miriam Graff, Bob Kotz, Bob Fox, Scott Beattie, Rudi Hargesheimer, Heidi Rigelman, John Green, Bill Dryborough, Ken Oelkers, Nancy Odden and Yafa Napadensky.

Field Checkers: Mike Anderson, Jim Erickson, Dave Geist, Rudi Hargesheimer, John Kohlstedt, Dick McDermott, Heidi Rigelman, Dick and Ella Slade, Anne and Peter Heegaard, Marilyn Vig, Andrew Slade, Bill Dryborough, Ted Tonkinson, Nancy Odden and Ken Oelkers.

Contributing Writers: Deb Shubat, Nancy Hylden, John Green, Lee Radzak, Andrew Slade, Rudi Hargesheimer, Catherine Long, John Kohlstedt, Jeanne Daniels, Anne McKinsey, Cindy Johnson-Groh, Janet Green and Tricia Ryan.

Maps: Matt Kania.

Book Production and Proofreading: Catherine Long, Tricia Ryan, Judy Gibbs, Kevin Roalson, Anne McKinsey, Rudi Hargesheimer, Tom Peterson, Kathy Hermes, Nancy Hylden, Jack Morris, Mark Wester, Sally Rauschenfels, Nancy Odden, Ann Possis, Ruth Hiland and Bill Dryborough.

Additional Support: Christie Printing Co., Minnesota Power, H.T. Klatzky and Associates, Inc. and Colorworks Graphics, Inc.

Made possible in part through the generous donations of Bill Hursh and Potlatch Corporation.

Foreword

What I remember best is squatting on a shoulder of rock, gazing out at the Poplar River Valley. The valley was lush and green and rolled on forever. Down the middle of it meandered the river itself, a reflection of horseshoe bends flowing cool and blue through the lowlands.

I was hot and sweaty from a morning on the trail, and I don't know how long I sat there. I couldn't tell you what I thought about, other than that it was one of the finest places I've ever shed a pack and let the breeze glide over my skin.

Doubtless hundreds of hikers have had the same feeling at a hundred different places along the Superior Hiking Trail.

It is that good.

We owe a large debt to the visionaries who conceived this trail and to Tom Peterson, who must have worn out several pairs of boots choosing its route. It is difficult to hike any distance on the trail without emerging in awe of Peterson's genius and dedication.

And now we have Andrew Slade and a whole crew of other volunteers to thank for this mile-by-mile companion piece to the trail itself. It was a book begging to be written, but which was going to require the spirit of a naturalist and the research of a scientist.

The book's production team, with the help of geologists, botanists, ornithologists, historians and camping experts, has given us a compendium of information about the Superior Hiking Trail. The book's format is hiker-friendly. Its detail is complete. And it fits in a backpack.

This book can help you park your car, arrange a shuttle, find water or find a camp. It'll tell you where you're likely to see a moose or to see Isle Royale, where you're treading in the voyageurs' footsteps and why the rock fractures the way it does along the Split Rock River.

The information in this guide will not weigh you down. It will answer a lot of your questions and free you to get on with the walking.

And maybe one day you'll find yourself doing what I was doing that July morning, what backpacking guru Colin Fletcher calls "sitting on a peak and thinking of nothing at all except perhaps that it is a wonderful thing to sit on a peak and think of nothing at all."

Good reading. Happy walking.

— SAM COOK

The Superior Hiking Trail

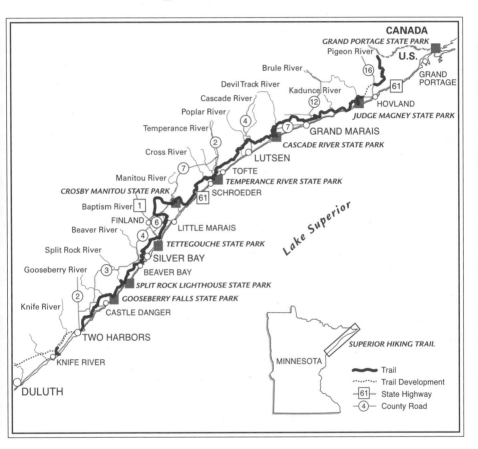

CANADA
GRAND PORTAGE STATE PARK
Pigeon River
U.S.
Brule River ⑯
GRAND PORTAGE
Devil Track River
Kaduncé River
61
Cascade River
⑫
HOVLAND
Poplar River
JUDGE MAGNEY STATE PARK
Temperance River
④
⑦
GRAND MARAIS
②
CASCADE RIVER STATE PARK
Cross River
LUTSEN
⑦
TOFTE
Manitou River
TEMPERANCE RIVER STATE PARK
CROSBY MANITOU STATE PARK
61
SCHROEDER
Baptism River 1
FINLAND ⑥
LITTLE MARAIS
Beaver River
④
TETTEGOUCHE STATE PARK
Split Rock River
SILVER BAY
Gooseberry River ③
BEAVER BAY
SPLIT ROCK LIGHTHOUSE STATE PARK
②
GOOSEBERRY FALLS STATE PARK
Knife River
CASTLE DANGER
TWO HARBORS
Lake Superior
KNIFE RIVER
SUPERIOR HIKING TRAIL
DULUTH
MINNESOTA
━━━ Trail
········· Trail Development
61 State Highway
④ County Road

S EE AN EAGLE, FLUSH A GROUSE. Rest in a cool cathedral of pine, shiver atop windswept vistas of Lake Superior. Behold rushing inland rivers, find a moss garden and nap in a field of spring wildflowers. Explore this magnificent landscape shaped by the greatest lake.

Table of Contents

History of the
Superior Hiking Trail

THE SUPERIOR HIKING TRAIL (SHT) WAS conceived in the mid-1980s as a long-distance footpath, modeled after the Appalachian Trail and other long trails, along the ridgeline adjacent to Lake Superior's North Shore from Duluth, Minnesota, to the Canadian border. As of April 2001, 235 miles of trail have been completed. With occasional small gaps, the SHT is completed from Two Harbors on the southwestern end to the Canadian border on the northeastern end.

The SHT is the realization of an ambitious plan fostered by a group of visionaries—federal, state and local government employees, artists, resort and business owners, and hiking enthusiasts—who in 1986 incorporated the Superior Hiking Trail Association (SHTA) and made the first request for state funding for trail construction. Three grants from the Legislative Commission on Minnesota Resources (LCMR), each covering a two-year period (1987–89, 1989–91 and 1991–93), were the principal source of funding for early trail construction. The LCMR funds were used primarily to pay the salary of Tom Peterson, the trail construction coordinator "on loan" from the Minnesota Department of Natural Resources, to buy materials, and to finance the crews from the Minnesota Conservation Corps and Lake County that have built substantial portions of the SHT. Other important funding sources have included the U.S. Forest Service, Lake County, and private donations, including corporate contributions.

The SHT was officially opened with a ceremonial "log-cutting" in July 1987, at Britton Peak on the Sawbill Trail, an event attended by federal, state, and local officials and dignitaries, in addition to the Trail's founders. In August 1990, the SHTA sponsored a "Halfway Celebration" at Gooseberry Falls State Park, commemorating the completion of nearly 140 miles of trail—approximately halfway to the goal of a continuous footpath from Duluth to the Canadian border. This celebration was the culmination of the SHTA's first sponsored backpacking trip, in which a dozen hikers trekked the completed Trail in twelve rigorous days. They were greeted by another impressive contingent of dignitaries and well-wishers at Gooseberry Falls State Park.

In September 1991, the Trail was the site of the first "Superior 100" endurance run, in which long-distance "ultra-marathon" runners from around the country competed in a 100-mile race. The race has been run every year since. For a few years in the mid-1990s there was also a snowshoe marathon held on the Trail in the winter.

The first documented through-hiker of the Trail was Paul Hlina in 1995. Paul raised $16,000 in pledges for the SHTA and Wilderness Inquiry as he hiked the length of the trail with crutches due to his paralyzed lower extremities.

Though a relative newcomer to the country's long-distance trails, and a toddler by comparision with its prototype and model, the Appalachian Trail (conceived in 1921 and completed, in its first layout, fifteen years later), the SHT has already won national recognition. It has been featured in countless regional publications and broadcasts and has been the subject of stories in national magazines, such as *Prevention, Walking* and *Backpacker* magazines. *Prevention* identified the Superior Hiking Trail as one of the twelve best trails in the national forests, and *Backpacker* Magazine rated it one of the ten best in the country.

General Description of the Trail

THE SUPERIOR HIKING TRAIL IS DESIGNED AS A footpath only, comprised mainly of an 18-inch treadway through a clearing approximately four feet in width. SHTA policy prohibits the use of motorized vehicles, mountain bikes and horses on the Trail. The steepness and narrowness of the SHT in most areas make it unsuitable for cross-country skiing, although snowshoe travel is possible.

For most of its length, the SHT is routed along the ridgeline overlooking Lake Superior. At its lowest point, the SHT goes along the lakeshore, which is 602 feet above sea level. At its highest point, in the hills of the Jackson Lake Road area, the SHT is 1829 feet above sea level and more than 1200 feet above Lake Superior. The SHT is characterized by ascents to rock outcroppings and cliffs, and descents into numerous river and creek valleys crossed by attractive and functional bridges. The SHT traverses a rich variety of terrain and habitat types. Woodlands of birch and aspen give way to stands of pine, fir and lush cedar groves. Grassy clearings, products of lumbering operations and forest fires, provide interesting variation from the more prevalent woodland scenes. Panoramic overlooks of Lake Superior, the Sawtooth Mountains and inland woodlands, lakes and rivers are abundant along the length of the SHT. At many points, the SHT follows rivers and creeks, often for distances of a mile or more, showcasing waterfalls and rapids, bends and deep gorges where thousands of years of rushing water have cut into layers of ancient volcanic bedrock. Steep portions of the SHT are accessed by log and stone stairways handcrafted by trail crews.

Hikers enjoy varied forest scenes. The gradual transition from oak, maple and basswood to the boreal forest of balsam, pines, spruces, cedar and tamarack is interrupted by regrowth forest of aspen and birch. Wildlife abounds: encounters with deer are common, as well as sightings of moose, beaver, black bear, eagles and grouse. Fortunate hikers will remember many varieties of songbirds. Wildflowers are especially prevalent in the spring, but some varieties are evident through the hiking season. Wild blueberries and raspberries provide a special midsummer treat at many points along the SHT.

The SHT crosses national forest and state park lands, state and county property, and private property. The SHT reaches the Canadian border where the Swamp River meets the Pigeon River, and along its route connects and traverses seven state parks. Many property owners—individuals and corporations, in addition to governmental units—have granted easements or permissions to cross their land for the construction of the SHT. In some areas, special restrictions apply as conditions of the permissions that have been granted on private lands. Please observe and obey all posted restrictions (such as requirements to stay on the trail through private property, or prohibitions on fires, camping or hunting). The privilege to use these private lands depends upon the cooperation of Trail users and their respect for the special restrictions.

The one constant feature of the SHT, and the characteristic that distinguishes it from other forest trails, is the presence of Lake Superior—the legendary lake Native Americans celebrated in song and story as "Gitche Gumme." Although the distance to the big lake varies considerably along the SHT, its presence is always felt. Sometimes the "lake effect" weather brings cool breezes and moisture in to shore, though in summer it may be 20 degrees warmer just over the ridge. The SHT features many spectacular views of the Lake, as well as many more subtle views through the trees, allowing the hiker an endless selection of spots to rest, lunch and meditate against the backdrop of Lake Superior's many moods and colors. From some vantage points, the Wisconsin/Michigan shoreline is visible on the horizon; other views feature islands—Isle Royale on the northern part of the SHT, and the Apostles on the southern end.

Lake Superior itself is 31,280 square miles—the largest freshwater lake in the world by area. It is 350 miles long and 160 miles wide at its farthest dimensions. Its average depth is 489 feet, and its maximum depth is 1333 feet. As a part of the Great Lakes shipping corridor, it is the inland terminus of a commercial shipping trade that reaches to the East Coast and across the Atlantic Ocean. After the ice departs Duluth harbor in spring, until sometime in January, the hiker can spot big vessels on the lake—the ore and grain freighters that carry midwestern exports to points east, and the "salties" that come from ports across the ocean. In the summer months when the lake is more often placid than angry, hikers can see sailboats, charter fishing boats and even small motorboats, canoes, and kayaks near the shore. The Lake's shipwrecks are legendary, and are documented at places such as the Split Rock Lighthouse visitor center and in books and paintings found in the many galleries and shops along the North Shore. Lake Superior, with its history and its beauty, gives the SHT a unique and unforgettable character.

ACCESSING AND USING THE TRAIL

The SHT is accessible directly from Minnesota Highway 61, on spur trails accessed from 61, or on many intersecting roads. Seven of the state parks along the North Shore (including Crosby-Manitou State Park, which is inland) are connected by the SHT and provide access to it. Along Highway 61, look for the brown signs with the Superior Hiking Trail logo on them. The distance between access points—most from five to ten miles apart—makes the SHT easily divisible into one-way day-hikes, accomplished by leaving a vehicle at the access point destination and shuttling to the next access point to begin the hike. If your party does not have two vehicles, shuttles may be arranged through the Superior Shuttle service at (218) 834-5511 or local resorts or outfitters. Numerous other possibilities exist for day hikes and loop hikes, some employing state park or national forest trails. Of course, a hike to a point on the trail with a return along the same trail is never a disappointment. The vista you missed over your shoulder on the way in is revealed in all its splendor on the way out. Rewarding day hikes are spotlighted in this book in the chapter, "Best of the Superior Hiking Trail," on page 43.

When planning a hike, allow one hour for every one-and-a-half to three miles. Day-hikers should carry a pack with adequate water (river and lake water along the SHT must be treated before it is consumed), snacks, sunscreen, bug repellent, toilet paper, compass, flashlight, and an extra clothing layer and raingear if conditions warrant. Remember that weather conditions can change rapidly; dark storm clouds and chilly winds sometimes move in quickly and unexpectedly on what began as a warm, cloudless day. If you plan to hike more than one or two hours, it is best to be prepared for weather changes.

Each season of the year offers its own rewards for the SHT hiker. Spring is a time for wildflowers, bird songs, and the unique color of emerging leaves. Summer brings the long hiking days and the sort of heat that makes a dip in one of the cool rivers all the more inviting. Fall is a symphony of colors and smells on the SHT, and the lack of biting insects makes it the friendliest time of year to hike. Fall also brings deer hunting season. Many sections of the SHT are closed during deer season. Check with the Superior Hiking Trail office or check the website for a list of closures. Signs are posted at trailheads to advise of trail closings. If you do hike on sections that are not posted closed, be sure to wear blaze orange clothing and stay alert.

Winter is a time of quiet magic on the SHT. While cross-country skiing would be nearly impossible, snowshoeing is increasingly popular. The SHTA offers group snowshoe hikes each winter. The primary differences between winter and non-winter use of the SHT are that snowshoeing takes much longer than hiking and some of the parking lots are not plowed. For more information, read *White Woods, Quiet Trails*, also by Ridgeline Press.

The SHT is also ideally suited for long-distance hiking. The hiker seeking an extended trip can hike the 235 miles of the SHT to its eastern end, then continue along the Border Route Trail, which in turn links with the Kekekabic Trail. These connections provide a multi-week adventure of over 300 miles, from near Ely in the west to near Grand Portage in the east, and then southwestward to Two Harbors on the Superior Hiking Trail.

For additional information about backpacking on the SHT and tips for overnight trips, see the "Backpacking Primer" chapter on page 33.

For the long-distance hiker who prefers more amenities, lodge-to-lodge hiking is available. You need carry only a daypack, since luggage is transported to your destination each day. For more information on lodge-to-lodge hiking, contact Boundary Country Trekking toll-free at (800) 322-8327.

This guidebook is designed to be a functional resource for you to plan your hiking adventure on the Superior Hiking Trail. The text is broken into segments, with a description of each trail section, and information on parking, access points and campsites. In addition, the highlights of each segment are featured—rivers, waterfalls, overlooks and other natural features. To enhance your hiking experience, information on human and natural history, both fact and legend, are also included, as well as explanations for some of the natural phenomena observed. At selected overlooks, the book tells you what you are seeing in the distance. Often when the SHT intersects state park and other trails, maps of those areas are provided to help you plan loop hikes. This information will maximize your enjoyment of the SHT.

Geology and Scenery
along the North Shore

MINNESOTA'S SHORELANDS OF LAKE SUPERIOR—the "North Shore"—is a land of rugged, forested hills, sweeping vistas of blue, green, autumn red and gold, and winter white, rocky headlands and crashing waves, cozy valleys and surging waterfalls. The dramatically beautiful landscape that we see today is a consequence of a geological history that goes back more than a billion years, into Late Precambrian time.

Regional geologic studies have shown that what is now the upper Great Lakes area had undergone several major periods of volcanism, intense deformation of the earth's crust, sedimentation and mountain-building. By about 1200 million years ago, erosion had eventually reduced the area to a low, rolling plain. There were no Great Lakes.

Then about 1100 million years ago the center of North America began to split apart as slow upwellings in the earth's stiff, plastic mantle (beneath the crust) began to melt, and huge volumes of molten rock (magma) leaked up to the surface along fissures in the crust. The present remains of this world-scale crustal feature, known as the Midcontinent Rift System, extend from southeastern Michigan north through the lower peninsula, westward through Lake Superior, and south-southwest beneath the Twin Cities and Iowa to northeast Kansas. Most of the magma was erupted as great, pancake-like flows of "flood basalt," of a composition similar to the modern or recent eruptions on Hawaii, Iceland or the Snake River Plain in Idaho. Hundreds of individual lava flows erupted, building up a sequence of layers up to 5 miles thick along the North Shore area and even thicker along the axis of the rift, now under the Lake.

As the crust was pulled apart, stretched and thinned, and magma erupted onto the surface from the mantle beneath, the center of the rift gradually subsided, leaving the rock layers tilted on the flanks towards the rift axis. Erosion during the last billion years has etched out these tilted layers to form the "Sawtooth Mountains" in Cook County. These are a series of long ridges with a relatively gentle southeast slope toward Lake Superior and a steep northwest slope, each one sculpted from a single huge lava flow.

Some basaltic magma never made it to the surface, but squeezed between older layers and solidified at various levels in the crust. When magma cools and crystallizes slowly it tends to produce larger crystals and the rocks thus formed (intrusive rocks) are generally more resistant when eventually exposed to erosion at the Earth's surface. A very large complex of intrusions, the Duluth Complex, underlies prominent highlands stretching from downtown Duluth southwestward past Spirit Mountain to Bardon Peak, and overlooks the St. Louis River valley and Wisconsin. (This same Duluth Complex also extends inland northward almost to Ely and eastward into Cook County.)

Smaller intrusions, mainly the dark rock diabase, squeezed in at higher levels within the lava-flow sequence. Some of these make up such prominent hills along the North Shore as Hawk Ridge at Duluth, Silver Cliff, most of the rugged highlands between Beaver Bay and Little Marais, Leveaux and Oberg Mountains and the ski hills at Lutsen. Diabase hills continue in the Hovland area and beyond Grand Portage, with the great ramparts of Hat Point, Mt. Josephine and the ridge beyond that overlooks Wauswaugoning Bay.

In some places these diabase magmas carried up huge blocks of a whitish rock called anorthosite, torn loose from the base of the crust about 25 miles beneath the surface. These anorthosites are very resistant to erosion, and now "hold up" such landmarks as Split Rock Lighthouse,

Mt. Trudee and other knobs in Tettegouche State Park, and the greatest of all, Carlton Peak at Tofte.

The great volumes of hot magma that worked their way up through the older crust melted some of it. This new magma had the composition of rhyolite or granite, with more silica and less iron than the basaltic magmas, and when it solidified it formed light-colored rocks in contrast to the dark basalt and diabase. Several very large rhyolite flows erupted; one of them forms the magnificent features of Palisade Head and Shovel Point in Lake County. Big rhyolites have also been eroded to form the deep gorges of the Devil Track, Kadunce, and Brule Rivers in Cook County, and of Split Rock River in Lake County.

For some as yet unknown reason, rifting and volcanism ended fairly abruptly without the continent coming completely apart to form a new ocean basin. The last major volcanic sequence can now be seen as the "backbone" of Isle Royale and of Keweenaw Point, far across the Lake in Michigan. The rift continued to sink for awhile, however, and streams washed sand, pebbles and mud into the slowly subsiding basin. Several miles of such sediment accumulated in the middle, some of which can be seen today on the Bayfield Peninsula and Apostle Islands, Wisconsin. Finally, over a period of perhaps 100 million years, the crust stabilized, and the buried sediments gradually hardened into rock. The most dramatic episode in Lake Superior history was over, and erosion by streams took over. But there was still no Lake Superior.

The last chapter in the saga of the North Shore's landscape is the Great Ice Age. Several times during the last two million years (most recently only about 14,000 years ago) great continental glaciers, up to one or two miles thick, built up and oozed southward from Canada. The great ice streams were mainly eroding the underlying rock, some of which had become deeply weathered. Moving southwestward, the Superior Lobe of the ice sheet carried debris (including volcanic rocks, agates and sandstone) from the North Shore area as far as the Twin Cities, the Minnesota River Valley, and even to Iowa. The ice found the sedimentary rocks in the middle of the old Midcontinent Rift System to be relatively easy to erode, and it excavated what was to be the Lake Superior basin well below sea level. As the glacier melted back about 11,000 years ago, it uncovered this great scooped-out depression which of course filled with water. Early stages (such as Glacial Lake Duluth) were several hundred feet higher than the present Lake, because the ice was still blocking the outlet. Look for rounded beach stones along the trail, high above the current Lake level. About 5000 years ago, Lake Superior as we know it today was well established. Since glaciation, the forests have covered the land, the North Shore rivers have been eroding their gorges, and waves have been making beaches and eating away at the shore cliffs and bluffs.

As you hike the SHT, remember this geologic history that has shaped the landscape. Look for evidence of volcanic activity, the "squeezed in" intrusions, glacial erosion and deposition, abandoned beaches far above the present Lake level and on-going geologic processes. Enjoy the geologic dimension!

Habitats of the
Superior Hiking Trail

THE SUPERIOR HIKING TRAIL FOLLOWS A corridor that is long enough to have members of three general vegetational groups along its length. One of these is hardwood forest that is at the northwestern limit of its distribution. These northern hardwoods, such as maple and oak, are concentrated in the highlands that form the setting for so much of the SHT. This group becomes less common as one travels northeastward from Duluth, and some species disappear completely by Cook County. The second group includes boreal species ranging across northern Minnesota. As the northern hardwoods thin out to the northeast, this second group becomes more prevalent along the SHT. The third group consists of species found primarily to the east along the U.S./Canada border but not ranging far to the north or south. The eastern white pine is typical of the border group.

Members from each of these forest "groups" exist side-by-side in a wide variety of different plant communities. By understanding where a tree comes from geographically, you can begin to make sense of why it is found in particular parts of the SHT. For example, you will find white spruce often in dark, cool valleys that better resemble northern habitat than the warmer, drier ridgetops. Glaciers deposited the rare deep soil along some of the ridges, providing a soil and a habitat for maples quite similar to that found in states further to the south.

THE NORTHERN HARDWOOD GROUP

Sugar maple is typically the most common tree in the northern hardwoods. Like many others in this group, it is associated with upper slopes, which are less frosty in the late spring. Sugar maple stands occur in all segments of the SHT. They were tapped for sugar by the Ojibway people. Sugar maple forests make fall hikes on the SHT glorious, turning hillsides into gold and red. Sugar maples can be identified by their leaves, whose well-known shape is seen on the Canadian flag.

Northern red oak is another northern hardwood. It is a large tree at the southwest end of the SHT. However, at the end of its range near the Lake/Cook County line, the oak is a small tree on rocky knobs. Its deep maroon leaves are among the last to drop in the fall.

Yellow birch can grow to the greatest diameter of any of the northern hardwoods. It may be identified in all seasons by scraping the bark from a twig and sniffing for the distinctive odor of wintergreen. These trees sometimes begin life on a dead log, which later rots away to leave a yellow birch growing "on stilts." This species often develops a hollow trunk, and so is an important site for animal denning or nesting.

Other less common members of this group include basswood, ironwood (hop hornbeam) and American elm.

THE BOREAL FOREST GROUP

Paper birch is extremely common throughout all but wet ground along the SHT. Its white bark and black twigs are more distinctive than its rather plain leaves. This tree requires sunny conditions for growth and fades from the scene as forest stands age and shade the forest floor. Droughts in the late 1980's have led to an extensive dieback of this species, especially near roads and clearcuts.

Balsam fir is a common tree in all parts of the SHT corridor. It seldom achieves great age or size before a storm knocks it down or spruce budworm kills it. Its needles are "flat and friendly," which distinguishes it from the "spiky" spruce. Crushing these needles will bring out an aroma reminiscent of winter holidays.

White spruce thrives throughout the SHT corridor where soils are deep enough. You can roll its needles between two fingers, and its bark is rougher than the balsam fir's bark. Large individuals are found here and there. On rock outcrops or in bogs, you may see black spruce, a smaller species. Black spruce is otherwise uncommon because of the scarcity of bogs near Lake Superior.

White cedar is common on both wet streams and dry rock outcrops, but only occasional on deep, well-drained soils. What these seemingly contradictory habitats have in common is a lower frequency of fire. White cedar, wherever you find it, is an important winter food for deer. You can identify this tree by its broad, flat, scaly needles and its stringy bark.

Balsam poplar is found predominantly in wet soil near streams. The long, sticky aromatic buds are distinctive, and perfume the woods during leaf out in the spring.

Mountain maple is a small tree or shrub with multiple stems. It grows in the understory of many kinds of trees on the uplands.

Jack pine is scarce along the North Shore in general. The damp summer and lack of expanses of coarse or shallow soils curtail the frequency of the fires on which this species depends.

THE BORDER GROUP

Several species have their ranges centered in the U.S./Canada border region to the east of Lake Superior. They overlap about equally with the northern portion of the hardwoods and the southern portion of the boreal forest.

Among these species is white pine. White pine is a distinctively majestic tree, with its feathery branches and dark trunk. On closer examination, you'll find that the needles come in clumps of five, as opposed to clumps of two with the red pine. This species was abundant over much of the North Shore region prior to logging. If you see a large, rotting stump on your hike, it is likely the remnant of a white pine that fell to the lumberjacks. The North Shore has a climate that is extremely favorable for the white pine blister rust fungus, so efforts to replant this species have been less successful here than in many other former pineries.

Red pine grows in scattered groves, often associated with rock out-crops. Like white pine, it was more abundant before the logging era, though not as common as its five-needled cousin. Disease does not currently pose a great threat to this species, which is also known as "Norway pine" and is the state tree of Minnesota.

Black ash is found mostly in damp ground, rarely with hardwoods on the uplands. It is abundant near many streams. This species seems to be the ultimate in caution, as it is the last to leaf out and the first to drop its leaves.

Heartleaf birch is a little-known tree that barely enters the North Shore from the east. It resembles paper birch, but has a rosy tinge to its bark. Also, it tends to have branches farther down the trunk than does paper birch, as heartleaf birch is more tolerant of shade. Despite the name, leaf shape is not easy to use for identification. In fact, some botanists list this as a variety of paper birch. This is the only tree species that is added as one proceeds northeastward on the SHT. Look for it in Cook and eastern Lake Counties.

Trembling aspen, also known as "popple" or "poplar," fits into none of the above groups and yet is one of the most common trees on the SHT. This species occupies more territory than any other North American tree, being found well to the north, south, east and west (with a hiatus in the Great Plains). It can be expected in the trail corridor wherever there are younger forests on deep soils. Old, shady stands are unlikely to have much aspen, although large trembling aspen are found in some places. This species increased greatly as the land was opened up by lumbering for pine and by the fires that sometimes followed.

This diversity of tree types parallels a diversity of wildflowers and other herbaceous growth. Minor variations in soil types can lead to major changes in the flora on the forest floor. Some stretches of rich soil will be covered with large-leaf aster and bluebead lily, while bare granitic rock may support some caribou moss and the polypody fern. Each month of spring, summer, and fall brings a new range of color and growth. As the snow melts in spring, look for violets, marsh marigold and wild lily-of-the-valley. As summer nears, the moccasin flowers and ladyslippers bloom, often in isolated and hard-to-find patches. In the heat of summer, watch for columbine, wild roses, buttercup and the towering cow parsnip. The onset of fall brings the asters and the goldenrods, which can bloom well into October.

Other flowers grow in distinct habitats, such as the water lilies and cattails in marshes, labrador tea and bog laurel in bogs, and twinflower, wintergreen and indian pipe in pine duff.

Overall, let these clues of trees and flowers guide you to an understanding of the varied terrain through which the SHT passes. On any given section of the trail you will pass through three, four or a dozen different habitats. Landforms, microclimates and succession determined these habitats, and the trees and other plants tell you fascinating stories about survival, and thriving, in the north woods.

Birds of the Lake Superior Highlands

ONE OF THE GREAT PLEASURES IN WALKING through the woods is being attuned to what other creatures are inhabiting the same piece of ground. Most forest animals are wary (at least those higher taxonomically than insects!), and their presence is not easily revealed. Birds, because they fly and they sing while nesting, are more conspicuous than most other vertebrates and thus add a dimension to the hike, whether you are teasing out a scolding ovenbird from the undergrowth or watching hawks migrate in the fall from one of the many overlooks.

The type of birdwatching you may experience along the Superior Hiking Trail depends on the character of the woods, the season of the year and the weather. Dedicated bird watchers with a penchant for listing notable species travel to the North Shore in search of gulls, sea ducks, and out-of-range migrants accidently appearing on the shore of Lake Superior. This search can be exciting sport, but an equally rewarding experience can be found in discovering what birds inhabit the forest that covers the hills back from shore. Now that the SHT provides good access to these woods, one can hike, look and listen for some of the approximately 100 species of birds that breed in the Lake Superior Highlands in summer. During both spring and fall migration, congregations of woodland birds are occasionally encountered, but the winter woods are virtually silent since most of the birds have gone to more southerly wintering grounds.

BIRDS OF PONDS AND STREAMS

- wood duck
- common goldeneye
- hooded merganser
- mallard
- blue-winged teal
- ring-necked duck
- great blue heron
- tree swallow
- spotted sandpiper
- kingfisher

RARE BREEDING BIRDS

- olive-sided flycatcher
- yellow-bellied flycatcher
- gray jay
- boreal chickadee
- Connecticut warbler
- Lincoln's sparrow

Lake Superior Highlands describes the ecoregion that the Superior Hiking Trail traverses. Ecoregions are defined by topography, climate, soils and vegetation. Habitat for birds is almost entirely determined by the vegetation, which on the forested hills of the Lake Superior Highlands is a mixture of deciduous and coniferous types with hardwood forest types predominant. Openings, either woodland ponds and streams, brushlands or cutovers, provide variety, as does an occasional boreal conifer bog or open ledge. These unusual habitats provide opportunities to see some rare nesting species.

Four species of raptors—turkey vulture, osprey, bald eagle, peregrine falcon—might be spotted flying over the forest from a rocky knob or pond edge. Two other species—red-tailed hawk and American kestrel—could be encountered nesting in forest that has been broken up by logging or other clearings. The deep-woods hawks—sharp-shinned, goshawk and broad-winged—are more numerous but rarely seen. The best evidence of their presence is the alarm cries given near a nesting site. Merlins are also very vociferous near the nest but are mostly found around big conifers along lakeshores.

Woodland ponds provide a place to see ducks, especially those that nest in tree cavities. A small colony of great blue herons or tree swallows might be discovered in a beaver pond and spotted sandpipers can be found bobbing along the rocks of open streams.

Where boreal conifer lowlands intersect the upland forest, a number of species confined to that special habitat can be located. Some of them, because they are rare breeders on a national scale, are much sought after by birders. Pockets of shrubby wetlands or water edges provide habitat for another group of species not otherwise present in the forested hills.

The greatest portion of the species present along the SHT, about three-fourths, are upland forest inhabitants, most of whom are only there for a short period of time during the breeding season (early May to early August). At least 73 species probably nest in these uplands, including the three hawks mentioned before, four owls (great horned, barred, long-eared, saw-whet), five other non-passerines (ruffed grouse, black-billed cuckoo, whip-poor-will, chimney swift, ruby-throated hummingbird), five woodpeckers and 56 passerines (songbirds).

A very few of these birds are permanent residents and might be found in winter woods on a snowshoe trek. The rest are here in the summer to take advantage of the abundant insects (mostly caterpillars) to feed their young, and the many diverse habitats provided by the mixed forest, including its cut-over patches and natural shrubby openings.

The diversity of the upland forest is the key to the richness of nesting species found there. Although most of the contiguous forest is deciduous, it is mixed with varying amounts of conifers, which sometimes form fairly pure stands. The age of the forest also varies from young, shrubby stands to big, old trees that form a dense canopy. Each habitat type has certain species that are adapted to what it provides for food and shelter, but some species are more specialized in their requirements than others. Those that are mostly restricted to

BIRDS OF SHRUBBY WETLANDS

- American woodcock
- alder flycatcher
- gray catbird
- golden-winged warbler*
- Tennessee warbler*
- northern waterthrush
- common yellowthroat
- Wilson's warbler*
- swamp sparrow

rare

PERMANENT RESIDENTS

- goshawk
- great horned owl
- barred owl
- downy woodpecker
- hairy woodpecker
- pileated woodpecker
- blue jay
- common raven
- black-capped chickadee
- red-breasted nuthatch
- pine siskin
- evening grosbeak

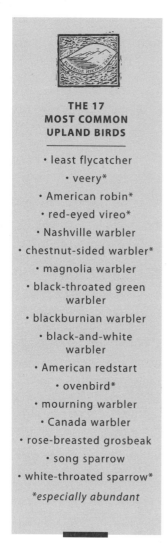

**THE 17
MOST COMMON
UPLAND BIRDS**

• least flycatcher
• veery*
• American robin*
• red-eyed vireo*
• Nashville warbler
• chestnut-sided warbler*
• magnolia warbler
• black-throated green
warbler
• blackburnian warbler
• black-and-white
warbler
• American redstart
• ovenbird*
• mourning warbler
• Canada warbler
• rose-breasted grosbeak
• song sparrow
• white-throated sparrow*

especially abundant

wetlands and openings have already been mentioned; and since these habitats are rare along the SHT, so are these species.

There are 73 species that are considered upland, forest-dependent breeding birds. The raptors (hawks and owls) have already been listed. They have large territories and their population density is quite low, so spotting one is a thrill. Most of the other forest nesting birds are more abundant, but small songbirds are not easily noticed in the thick vegetation. About half of the woodland birds belong to just four taxonomic families: thrushes (5 species), vireos (4 species), warblers (17 species) and sparrows/finches (11 species).

The summer hiker who is not a birder is probably amazed that the woods contain so many species. Except for the dawn chorus (starting from 4:30 a.m. when even a dedicated nature explorer is likely asleep), their presence is only revealed by scolding chips or an occasional burst of song. To really appreciate the birds along the SHT, learning the songs, at least of some of the common species, will add immense pleasure to the hiking experience. The intense singing period is at the height of the nesting cycle, which is a very short time from early June to early July. There are some good, commercial birding tapes that aid in learning bird songs, but the best way is spotting the songster with binoculars and identifying it while it sings.

Two species are much prized by birders because the North Shore forest is the only place in Minnesota that they are known to regularly breed: Philadelphia vireo and black-throated blue warbler.

Weather is always a variable in bird-watching and windy days slow down song and other bird activity considerably. However, in the fall it is on those glorious days with a good northwest wind, following the passage of a cold front, that hawk-watching is the most rewarding. Hawks and other day-time migrants are funneled along the shore of Lake Superior and use the updrafts from the hills to aid them in their flight. The bulk of the hawk migration is from about the 10th of September through the 10th of October, but eagles and northern raptors can be seen on days with good migration weather through early December.

The overlooks along the SHT provide opportunities for witnessing this migration, although concentrations are not nearly as large as near Duluth. Other birds migrate in flocks, usually in the morning, and can be seen in numbers in a wide band along the North Shore in the fall: blue jay, American crow, common raven, American robin, cedar waxwing and seven species of winter finches.

Both spring (May) and fall (September through early October), flocks of small birds can be encountered, usually spotted feeding intensely in the treetops (vireos and warblers) or flushed while walking along the trail (thrushes and sparrows). Their presence depends on the weather they have encountered during migration. Local breeding birds also congregate in foraging flocks after the nesting season and before they set out on their long-distance migration to the tropics. They are often joined by the permanent residents, chickadees and woodpeckers, who usually announce their presence by their flocking calls.

Each hiking trip, depending on time and place, can produce a different experience with the birds in the woods. Storing up these moments expands the memory of the event and can also add to the knowledge of the birds of the Lake Superior Highlands.

Animals of the
Superior Hiking Trail

DESCRIBING THE ANIMAL LIFE OF THE North Shore and the Superior Hiking Trail is challenging because of its great variety. Fortunately, for the sake of brevity, it's possible to make some distinctions. First of all, there are animals in the official sense, that is, things that move and eat other things. But then there are "animals," generally fuzzy things with one set of eyes. Is that black fly biting your earlobe an animal? Yes, indeed. But a lot of people would rather swat the black fly while looking for "real" animals like a deer, wolf or turtle. Insects, reptiles, fish, and amphibians are all animals but, due to space, will receive only short notice here. And the birds of the Superior Hiking Trail are covered in the previous chapter. This chapter will mostly cover the mammals of the SHT.

As you hike, you may encounter animals of three basic types:

1) Small animals which are common but seldom seen;

2) Medium-size animals which are somewhat common and often seen; and

3) Medium-to-large, generally carnivorous animals which are rare, wide-ranging and also seldom seen.

On your typical day hike you probably won't see a lot of animals besides birds and insects. That's not because they aren't there. But unless you have the eyes of a hawk, you'll likely miss the mice and shrews that cruise the underbrush. And unless you are quiet and lucky, you probably won't see a wolf. However, white-tail deer, the snowshoe hare and the red squirrel, among others, are animals that are commonly seen along the SHT.

Although you may not see any large mammal, you will undoubtedly see some evidence of their passing. They are out there. Many mammals are active during the morning and evenings, but rest during the day. The white-tail deer you see bounding through the forest may have been resting from a busy night of feeding before you startled it. If you want to learn about the animals of the SHT, you will do better to look for evidence rather than the animal itself.

If you do look for animal signs, you won't be disappointed. In a muddy section of the SHT, look for tracks of deer, moose and wolves, animals likely to use the SHT as an easy path through remote woods. Scat (animal feces) is another obvious sign, and becomes more obvious when an animal uses scat to mark territory. When there is a prominent, bare rock near the trail, look for wolf or coyote scat (told by the ropy texture, hair and bone chip content) or that of the fisher or marten (which is long, slender, and dark). All these mammals use scat to mark their territory with both its sight and smell. Other signs of large animals include bark rubbings by male moose and deer, deer and moose beds in grassy areas, and nests. If this sort of animal watching interests you, bring a book such as Peterson's *A Field Guide to Animal Tracks*. There are some fascinating stories to be read in the woods.

Small animals that are common but seldom seen

This category includes all the shrews, voles, mice and little weasels. These animals are used to fleeing at the sound (or feel) of danger. You'll see their trails crossing above or sometimes below the SHT. In open areas, look for the birds like kestrels who are looking, in turn, for these little creatures. At dusk, in a campsite, a woodland deer mouse or short-tailed shrew might try to get into your food or clean up your dinner scraps.

These small creatures play important roles in ecosystems as primary consumers and carnivores (mostly of insects). They also aerate and enrich the soil with their tunnels. For every one large, dramatic carnivore in the food web there are thousands of little creatures, all doing their part to keep the cycles flowing. And in case you are fortunate enough to encounter one, remember that the short-tailed shrew is one of only two North American mammals with a venomous bite.

Medium-to-large size animals that are somewhat common and often seen

• WHITE-TAIL DEER

Although the deer is a common resident now, a century ago there were hardly any here. Instead there were woodland caribou, which thrived on lichens and moss of the primordial forest. Now, with logging and other habitat changes, the caribou are only in Canada (with the notable exception of a caribou wandering in Hovland in the winter of 1980-81). Deer congregate along the North Shore in winter and early spring, where snowfall is lighter and melts sooner, making food more accessible and travel easier. The Jonvik deer yard near Lutsen is one of the largest deer yards in the state. For two weeks in the fall, generally the first and second weeks in November, deer are hunted all along the Superior Hiking Trail, so wear bright colors.

• MOOSE

Count yourself fortunate if you encounter one of these gentle giants on your hike. You'll increase your luck if you look carefully in the low, wet areas near the SHT. Look for a brown boulder moving among the lily pads. In general, deer and moose populations do not intermix. The deer carry a flatworm which doesn't harm the deer but is fatal to the moose. Moose droppings are thumb-size, light brown pellets, found in large piles. Moose tracks have the same double half-moon shape of the deer, but are at least twice as long. Some classic moose habitat along the Superior Hiking Trail includes Jonvik Creek and the wetlands around Grand Portage.

• BLACK BEAR

The black bear is an incredible survivor. It uses every trick in the book to survive the north woods. Bears have one of the most diverse natural diets around, including your food bag if you're not careful. Bears' diet follows the season: when the blueberries are ripe, they gorge on blueberries, and likewise with the hazelnuts or other edibles. When there's no more fresh food, around the end of September, bears begin to go into torpor, a sort of intermittent hibernation. The SHT passes near a grove of oak trees in Tettegouche State Park that is a magnet for bears from 50 miles around when the acorns are ripe in the fall. Treat these creatures with the respect they deserve—that includes putting your food far out of reach when you're camping.

• WEASELS
You may not see a weasel, but weasels are mammals worth noting. There is a whole family of weasels of all different sizes, all with the same mode of survival: chase and kill. The short-tailed weasel, or ermine, chases mice; the fisher and marten chase larger prey such as squirrels and hares. You'll be thrilled if you ever witness one of their chases. In the winter, look for their distinctive bounding tracks in the snow.

• SNOWSHOE HARE
Depending on their population cycles, you may see lots of hares or you may see none. Even if they are around, you have to look carefully. With their changing coat, they are always well camouflaged. They prefer thickets of shrubs and short trees, which give them plenty of cover from predators such as great-horned owls and lynx.

• RED SQUIRREL
The sound of a red squirrel defending its territory is one of the standard anthems of the north woods. That sharp, rattling "chirrrr" is the squirrel's way of telling you to beat it. Each squirrel defends a territory of about a 200-yard diameter circle. If the summer and fall harvests are good, the squirrel will store up to 14,000 food items in this territory, including cones, mushrooms and nuts (the mushrooms are hung on tree bark where they can dry). Red squirrels can become overly friendly in campsites if they are fed by hikers.

• BEAVER
As the SHT works its way up and down hills and across streams, it is bound to take you through the work of the beaver. Sometimes, though, you won't even notice. The beaver, with its propensity to change the environment to suit its needs (like another mammal, *Homo sapiens*),

has been around long enough that its ponds have turned into forests. Some particularly spectacular beaver ponds can be found near Sawmill Creek and on Jonvik Creek, where the SHT crosses the creek on a beaver dam, as well as along the upper reaches of the Gooseberry River.

Medium-to-large, generally carnivorous animals that are rare, wide-ranging and also seldom seen

• TIMBER WOLF

Along the North Shore, starting northeast of Two Harbors, there are numerous packs of wolves. This is, however, the fringe of their population. The traffic and development of Highway 61 keeps most wolves inland, though the Superior Hiking Trail leads through some prime wolf territory. To see a wolf you would have to know their travel paths and disguise yourself from sight or smell. Look for scat and tracks along the SHT, also the occasional kill site of a well-broken-up deer carcass. The presence of the wolves is a testimony to the wildness of the land through which you are travelling.

• COYOTE

Where there aren't wolves along the North Shore, there are likely to be coyotes. Wolves defend their territories from coyotes, but as the edge of wolf range fluctuates, so does the coyote range. Coyotes are smaller than wolves but larger than foxes, and can be identified by their large ears and bouncing gait. They're more of a "suburban" animal, more accustomed to human presence. Like wolves, they have eerie, though distinct, howling sessions.

• LYNX AND BOBCAT

Solitary hunters, these wild cats prey mostly on the snowshoe hare, and so their populations vary with the hare's. The bobcat is at the northern edge of its range and the lynx is at its southern edge. The lynx travels 3–6 miles a night in search of food, but success is less than fifty-fifty each night. Both cats have ranges rather than territories, which means they can overlap with others of the same species and are not generally defended. Another even bigger cat, the mountain lion, has been spotted in recent years in St. Louis and Cook Counties.

Other animals on the Superior Hiking Trail

Insects are animals, right? If you're out in May through September, you'll likely encounter some of these. Not all of them are out to bite you, either. But some will try. Watch for black flies in May and June, various species of mosquito from May to September, and deer and horse flies in July and August. Look for dragonflies, leeches, colorful beetles, and aquatic insects in the streams. Also in the streams you'll find brook trout, and a host of frogs, turtles, and salamanders.

The animal life along the North Shore is a significant part of what makes the SHT so special. With careful observation, you'll find that there is a world of creatures as wild and dramatic as the cliffs and mountains of the shore. As you wind your way through different habitats, keep an eye out for the "locals." Either a sighting or a sign will let you in on part of the great mystery of this land.

General North Shore History

THE FIRST PEOPLE TO ENTER THE NORTH SHORE region arrived around 10,000 years ago. These Native Americans, called Paleo-Indians, entered the region during the final retreat of the Wisconsin Glaciation. As the Superior ice lobe melted back to the northeast, it blocked the present outlet of Lake Superior, causing lake levels to rise above their present level by up to 450 feet.

This enlarged Lake Superior is known as Glacial Lake Duluth, and in many areas the ancient shoreline closely follows the ridgeline that much of the Superior Hiking Trail now follows. The Paleo-Indians were big game hunters of caribou, bison, musk ox and possibly mammoth. In all probability, these hunters followed the shoreline of this lake of glacial meltwater along these present-day ridge tops.

The Old Copper Culture followed the Paleo-Indian cultural tradition around Lake Superior and existed from about 5000 years ago until about 2000 years ago. During this time the Indians used raw native copper, found on Isle Royale and in northern Michigan, hammering it into tools. Occasionally copper artifacts, in the form of spear points, knives, and fish hooks, are found along the North Shore. If you find copper or stone tools, contact the state archaeologist in Duluth at (218) 726-7154. These finds are very rare and the information will add to the knowledge of this early history.

Many waves of Indian people inhabited the North Shore prior to European contact. The first Europeans, French explorers and fur traders, first reached the Lake Superior country about 1620. At that time, the Ojibway (also called Anishinabe or Chippewa) inhabited the eastern end of the lake as far west as the Upper Peninsula of Michigan. Their culture centered at the rapids at the outlet of the big lake. By 1650 the French had encountered the Dakota, or Sioux, at the head of the lake. Along the North Shore lived the Assiniboine and the Cree. As the fur trade moved west over the next 100 years, so did the Ojibway, displacing by 1750 the Dakota, the Assiniboine, and the Cree, who moved farther to the west and north.

By 1780, the Europeans had established fur trading posts at the mouth of the St. Louis River and at Grand Portage. The Ojibway were firmly established on the western end of the lake and in northeastern Minnesota. Both Europeans and Ojibway navigated their frail birch bark canoes along the rugged North Shore between these two important sites of early commerce and, although the Ojibway did have foot trails heading inland at different points along the shore, the early traders had little reason to leave the lake and explore the adjacent uplands.

In 1854, the Ojibway signed the Treaty of La Pointe, which opened up northeastern Minnesota to mineral exploration and settlement. The first permanent settlement was a group of Germans from Ohio who settled at Beaver Bay in 1856. The late 1800s saw a rise of commercial herring fishing along the North Shore, and it was said that nearly every cove harbored at least one fisherman's shanty.

Across Lake Superior, Michigan lumber barons had cut most of the big stands of virgin white pine in Michigan by 1890. They then set their sights on Lake Superior's North Shore. Between 1890 and 1910, millions of board feet of red and white pine were cut from the hills along the North Shore. Temporary railroads transported the logs down to the Lake where they were rafted up and towed by tugboat to sawmills in Duluth, Superior, Bayfield and Ashland. Today many of these old railroad grades—most used only for one or two seasons—are still visible. In places, the Superior Hiking Trail either crosses or follows some of these straight and level grades such as the Alger, Nestor and Merrill-Ring grades.

Ever since northeastern Minnesota was opened to exploration, mining has had an active history on the North Shore. Small, unproductive copper explorations began along some of the rivers in the 1850's and 1860s. In 1884, high-grade iron ore from the Iron Range in northeastern Minnesota started shipping from the huge ore docks in Two Harbors on ore boats bound for the mills on the lower lakes.

At the turn of the century a new company was formed in Two Harbors, Minnesota Mining and Manufacturing. Known today as 3M, the company planned to mine an abrasive rock, believed to be corundum, at Crystal Bay near the mouth of the Baptism River. At the same time, the North Shore Abrasives Company was formed to mine the same type of rock from a location near Split Rock. In both cases the rock was found to be too soft to serve as an abrasive, and mining operations were discontinued by 1906.

Taconite, a material refined from low-grade iron ore, was produced in the 1950s from mines on the Minnesota Iron Range. Taconite pellets continue to be processed and shipped to refineries on the lower Great Lakes from Duluth, Two Harbors, Silver Bay and Taconite Harbor. Operational railroad tracks crossed by the SHT connect the mines near Ely, Babbitt and Hoyt Lakes with these shipping points along the North Shore.

It is obvious to anyone visiting the North Shore that tourism and recreation have had, and continue to have, a major impact on local development. As early as 1910, when Split Rock Lighthouse was built, the lightkeeper recorded that tourists began visiting the light station by sailboat. Even though a one-lane wagon road was built between certain points along the shore in the 1890s, the present North Shore highway was not completed between Duluth and the Canadian border until 1924. When the highway was completed, camping and cabin resorts sprang up along the shore. Seven state parks were set aside and protected, joined most recently by the eighth, Grand Portage State Park. Today, hikers on the Superior Hiking Trail can still look upon many of the same unspoiled vistas that the Native Americans and the first French explorers saw.

For more information on the cultures and peoples that have inhabited the North Shore, visit the Cook County Historical Society, the Lake County Historical Society, or the Split Rock Lighthouse visitor center.

About the Superior Hiking Trail Association

THE SUPERIOR HIKING TRAIL ASSOCIATION (SHTA) is a Minnesota non-profit corporation whose members are dedicated to the completion, preservation and promotion of the Superior Hiking Trail. The original members of the SHTA were the visionaries— federal and state government representatives and local North Shore resort and business owners—who incorporated the SHTA and obtained the first funding to see their vision become a reality. From this small group, membership has grown to approximately 3000, including members in 37 states, Canada and four other foreign countries.

The SHTA has a few paid staff members working in the office/store in Two Harbors. Apart from some work performed on contract, the remainder of the work of the SHTA is done by volunteers. A board of directors consisting of members from a variety of locations, careers, avocations, and age groups meets bimonthly on the North Shore to make policy decisions for the SHTA. Committees of SHTA members are responsible for the substantive work of the association, including trail maintenance, product sales, planning organized hikes, and publications.

The most visible activities of the SHTA are the popular organized hikes scheduled throughout the hiking season, including wintertime snowshoe hikes. Hosted by SHTA members and featuring leaders with interpretive skills, such as naturalists, geologists, photographers, and historians, most of the SHTA-sponsored events are one-way day hikes with shuttle service allowing hikers to leave their cars at the final destination and hike to them at their own pace. The SHTA's hiking program also features backpacking trips of several days' duration. SHTA members also have the opportunity to attend the annual business meeting, scheduled in May, and to participate in a weekend full of hiking, fun, and comraderie planned around the meeting.

Much of the trail was built by crews hired from the local communities and from the Minnesota Conservation Corps (MCC). MCC crews will likely continue to help maintain the SHT. Additional maintenance is provided through a system of volunteers: some have taken responsibility for the upkeep of particular sections; others participate in scheduled maintenance hikes. Scout troops, outdoors clubs, and other organizations have undertaken trail maintenance responsibilities. Individual hikers and groups can give something back to the trail by volunteering to help with trail maintenance. The SHTA will gladly provide you with information on how you can help.

The SHTA provides its members with maps, *The Ridgeline* newsletter, the opportunity to participate in organized hikes and other activities, and the knowledge that through membership fees they are helping to preserve and protect a precious resource—the Superior Hiking Trail. For information on membership, SHTA activities, trail maintenance or other volunteer activities, contact the SHTA office at (218) 834-2700, mail us at P.O. Box 4, Two Harbors, MN 55616-0004, or visit our website at www.shta.org. If you're in Two Harbors, drop by the office and store at 731 Seventh Ave., two blocks west of Dairy Queen.

A Superior Hiking Trail Backpacking Primer

ACKPACKING ALLOWS YOU TO EXPERIENCE the wilderness intimately and up close. While this chapter will help hikers enjoy the trail fully and with comfort, experience is the best teacher. Get out there and do it! The goal is to enjoy the walk and the camp.

GENERAL HIKING TIPS

The Superior Hiking Trail is particularly well-suited to the novice backpacker. One is never far from the road, the grocery store and comfortable resorts if the weather or your enthusiasm turns, tempting you to bail out. Plan your trip accordingly. Plan escape routes to civilization ahead of time. Make your trip a combination of backpacking and resorting and enjoy the best of both worlds!

Regardless of whether you are hiking for a week or an hour, it is always a good idea to let someone know your plans. Tell someone where you plan to hike and when you plan to arrive; then check in when you return. The trail is not patrolled, so your safety or rescue in an emergency may depend on this common-sense precaution.

Backpackers will find back-country camping spots, most near a water source, every five to eight miles along much of the SHT. The state parks also have camping facilities. Multi-group campsites are found in high-use areas and are meant first for larger groups. You should be pre-

BACKPACKER'S CAMPING EQUIPMENT LIST: Personal items

- Sturdy, comfortable hiking boots
- 2-3 pairs wool socks
- 2 pairs liner socks, silk or synthetic
- Long underwear
- Wool or pile pants
- Lightweight pants, shorts, short and long-sleeved shirts
- Sweater or pile jacket
- Rain jacket or poncho
- Rain pants
- Hat, gloves, gaiters if any probable snow
- Bandana, small towel
- Swim suit (same as shorts, perhaps)
- Sleeping bag
- Stuff sacks
- Foam pad
- Internal or external frame pack
- Sleeping bag lash straps

pared to share these sites with other hikers. If a designated campsite is already full, backpackers should move to the next site or ask to share the site. Use only designated sites. Within the state parks backpackers must register and pay regular camping fees.

UNDERSTANDING THE BACKPACKER'S CHECKLIST

The chief nemesis of the sore-hipped, aching-shoulder backpacker is, of course, weight. What to pack, how much to pack, and where in the pack to put it is often-requested information. Use the lists presented here for ideas of what to bring, not as a mandatory agenda. When all is packed, your backpack should weigh 30–50 pounds, no more! The necessity of lightweight gear may preclude using much of the camping equipment you may already own. Use what you have that is lightweight, borrow from friends or rent the gear you need if you are unsure that backpacking is for you.

Following are brief explanations of some items noted on the checklist.

Hiking boots. For safe packing and assured ankle support you will need lightweight, over-the-ankle, lug-soled boots, preferably waterproof. Wet boots are usually sloppy fitting and lead to blisters and stumbles. Waterproofness is found in Gore-Tex (or similar material) and full-grain leather boots.

Socks. The most important criterion is fit. Wear what fits well in your boots. A synthetic liner will "wick" moisture away from your foot.

A wet foot is a cold foot. Wearing liner socks along with thicker wool socks helps disperse the friction that causes blisters. Let the socks rub against each other, not you.

Long underwear. Synthetic underwear keeps the wearer dry and warm. Leave the long underwear at home if you don't expect cool days or cold nights.

Sweater. Polyester or nylon pile sweaters serve the same function as a wool sweater. They keep you drier, are less bulky and weigh less than wool.

Rain jacket and pants. Make sure they work. At a minimum they should keep you dry when it's raining. Better yet, they should be something you can wear as an outer shell to break the wind. In this case it should be a "waterproof/breathable" fabric.

Other pants, shirts, shorts. You should carry a minimum amount of these. You can change into clean clothes at the car.

Sleeping bags. Better quality down bags are very lightweight, low bulk, retain their loft for many years, and offer the greatest comfort range—from cold nights to hot, humid nights. Synthetic fill bags are heavier, bulkier, and offer less range of comfort than down bags, but will offer more warmth when wet. They are not as resilient as down bags, tending to lose loft over time.

Personal items, CONTINUED

- Compass
- Map/trail guide/ map case
- Water bottle or canteen
- Eating utensils: cup, bowl, plate, spoon, fork
- Sharp knife
- Flashlight or head-lamp, extra batteries
- Waterproof matches or butane lighter
- Candle or firestarter
- Sunglasses
- Sunscreen
- Insect repellent (mosquitoes, ticks, black flies)
- First aid kit, with extra moleskin or foot care kit
- Toothbrush, comb, biodegradable soap, etc.
- 50' nylon cord
- Spare pack parts/ sewing items
- Personal snacks or lunch food
- Day pack for side hikes

Stuff sacks. Use the one the sleeping bag comes in filled with clothing as a pillow. Use another inexpensive one for food, another for the cookset. Your sleeping bag should be kept in a truly waterproof stuff sack.

Pack. You'll want one that comfortably transfers weight to the frame of your body and onto your legs. It can be an external frame pack, one that puts most of the weight on your hips, or it can be an internal frame pack, one that is designed to disperse weight evenly over your entire back and hips. The external frame packs have the disadvantage of being less stable, prone to awkwardly shifting at just the wrong time. Internal frame packs accomplish their superior stability by offering many more complex design features. Comfortable ones tend to be much more expensive than good external frame packs.

Tent. Lightweight, sturdy, dry…is that too much to ask? Look for freestanding designs. They are easy to pitch and shed wind well. The sturdiest have heavy duty fabrics and multiple pole crossovers creating a geodesic structure. Conversely, an ultralight tent will have lightweight fabrics and few if any geodesic features. A compromise between ultimate toughness and weight savings is necessary for most of us. Dryness is related to fabric quality, sealed seams and ventilation. A good tent will not only keep rain out, but also let your body heat and vapor out from inside. Look for design features that allow for venting, even during a downpour. A tarp sized a bit smaller than your tent floor can be put under the tent to protect the floor.

Stoves. Lightweight one-burner stoves are mandatory. The easiest to use are those with fuel in sealed canisters, such as butane, iso-butane or other fuels. The canister plugs into the burner and with a twist of the knob and one match you've got a flame. Unfortunately these stoves often don't put out enough heat and they can work poorly in subfreezing weather. Gasoline burning stoves are more versatile; you carry the fuel in a refillable fuel bottle. This is more ecologically sound and your stove will work in all weather conditions. The disadvantage of these stoves is that they are sometimes fickle, and may require preheating with fire paste or liquid fuel. Look for ones that both simmer well and bring water to a quick boil.

Food. Be prepared to carry lots of extra weight if you want to have fun making meals from scratch. The lightweight alternatives, freeze-dried foods, are very easy to prepare, and also relatively expensive. Instant soups are inexpensive and very low in weight and bulk.

Lunch foods should be low in liquid content, yet durable (oranges are heavy and full of juice, bananas bruise). Bagels can withstand heaps of abuse. Nuts, cheeses, salami, jams, peanut butter, and cream cheese are all good bets. Also try energy bars and sports drinks.

Breakfasts can be as simple as oatmeal or granola with powdered milk. Pancakes are excellent if you don't need to get moving quickly.

Water. All drinking water must be boiled, filtered or chemically treated. Iodine tablets are the best chemical treatment but the water will taste of iodine. Backcountry filters are considered to be the best option because they remove all harmful bacteria, giardia, and funny tastes. A purifier is a filter with chemicals added to kill viruses, a great choice if you ever have to travel to third world countries. Look for filters or purifiers that are self-cleaning and easy to use.

Fun accessories. Some things aren't essential but are fun to take along anyway. Bring one or two. Examples: boomerangs, Frisbees, Hacky Sacks, cards, games, harmonicas, chairs, books, solar showers, cameras, film, compasses, altimeters, etc.

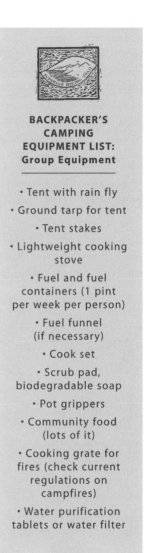

BACKPACKER'S CAMPING EQUIPMENT LIST: Group Equipment

- Tent with rain fly
- Ground tarp for tent
- Tent stakes
- Lightweight cooking stove
- Fuel and fuel containers (1 pint per week per person)
- Fuel funnel (if necessary)
- Cook set
- Scrub pad, biodegradable soap
- Pot grippers
- Community food (lots of it)
- Cooking grate for fires (check current regulations on campfires)
- Water purification tablets or water filter

Packing the pack. Get everything as close to your center of gravity as possible. When carrying 30–50 pounds, this spot will be directly behind your spine and near your shoulder blades. Pack your sleeping bag at the bottom, heavier things behind your shoulders, and lighter things

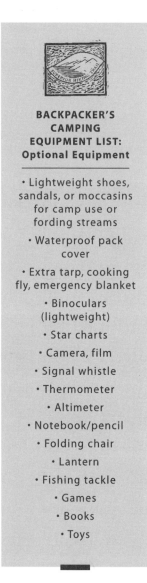

BACKPACKER'S CAMPING EQUIPMENT LIST: Optional Equipment

- Lightweight shoes, sandals, or moccasins for camp use or fording streams
- Waterproof pack cover
- Extra tarp, cooking fly, emergency blanket
- Binoculars (lightweight)
- Star charts
- Camera, film
- Signal whistle
- Thermometer
- Altimeter
- Notebook/pencil
- Folding chair
- Lantern
- Fishing tackle
- Games
- Books
- Toys

above your shoulders. Pack as little as possible to the far left or right of your spine.

No pack is truly waterproof. You should use waterproof stuff sacks for your gear and/or use pack liners (garbage bags work) or pack covers if you want bone-dry performance.

Bears and other raiders. Never take any food into your tent at night. Hoist all of your food and garbage in its stuff sack into a tree. It should end up hanging 10 feet off the ground and 5 feet from the tree trunk. Use a rock tied to the end of your rope to get the rope slung over a high sturdy branch, then tie the food bag to one end of the rope. Pull the other end until the bag is suspended, then tie off that end to the tree trunk. When leaving camp be sure to pack out all food debris. Any garbage left in the campsite is a potential attraction for bears. Once a bear finds food at a campsite, he is likely to return and could cause a problem for other campers using the site.

Synopsis. Backpacking can be as much work or as little work as you make it. If you can carry a minimum of frills, your pack can weigh less than 30 pounds for a one-week trip and you will enjoy walking ten miles or more per day. Or…you can bring all manner of heavy gear, which allows for deluxe camping but sore shoulders after only six miles of walking. The perfect compromise is somewhere in between for most of us.

Minimum Impact Trail Use: *Leave No Trace*

THE SUPERIOR HIKING TRAIL HAS BEEN designed to minimally alter the environment. It can be argued that its very existence, and this guidebook's encouragement of more discovery and usage of the SHT, is detrimental to the wilderness ecosystems through which it passes. Conversely, the exposure of this pristine environment to a multitude of people may develop an increased awareness and appreciation of the environment for those people. Educating the public about wilderness values is, in fact, a goal of the Superior Hiking Trail Association.

The SHTA adheres to the principles of the "Leave No Trace Outdoor Ethic." Those principals are listed below.

LEAVE NO TRACE PRINCIPLES:

<u>PLAN AHEAD AND PREPARE</u>

- Know the regulations and special concerns for the area you'll visit.
- Prepare for extreme weather, hazards, and emergencies.
- Schedule your trip to avoid times of high use.
- Visit in small groups. Split larger parties into groups of 4–6.
- Repackage food to minimize waste.
- Use a map and compass to eliminate the use of rock cairns, flagging or marking paint.

TRAVEL AND CAMP ON DURABLE SURFACES

- Durable surfaces include established trails and campsites, rock, gravel, dry grasses or snow.

- Protect riparian areas by camping at least 200 feet from lakes and streams. Good campsites are found, not made. Altering a site is not necessary.

In popular areas:

- Concentrate use on existing trails and campsites.

- Walk single file in the middle of the trail, even when wet or muddy.

- Keep campsites small. Focus activity in areas where vegetation is absent.

DISPOSE OF WASTE PROPERLY

- Pack it in, pack it out. Inspect your campsite and rest areas for trash or spilled foods. Pack out all trash, leftover food, and litter.

- Deposit solid human waste in catholes dug 6 to 8 inches deep at least 200 feet from water, camp, and trails. Cover and disguise the cathole when finished.

- Pack out toilet paper and hygiene products.

- To wash yourself or your dishes, carry water 200 feet away from streams or lakes and use small amounts of biodegradable soap.

- Scatter strained dishwater.

LEAVE WHAT YOU FIND

- Preserve the past: observe, but do not touch, cultural or historic structures and artifacts.

- Leave rocks, plants and other natural objects as you find them.

- Avoid introducing or transporting non-native species.

- Do not build structures, furniture, or dig trenches.

MINIMIZE CAMPFIRE IMPACTS

- Campfires can cause lasting impacts to the backcountry. Use a lightweight stove for cooking and enjoy a candle lantern for light.

- Where fires are permitted, use established fire rings, fire pans, or mound fires.

- Keep fires small. Only use sticks from the ground that can be broken by hand.
- Burn all wood and coals to ash, put out campfires completely, then scatter cool ashes.

RESPECT WILDLIFE

- Observe wildlife from a distance. Do not follow or approach them.
- Never feed animals. Feeding wildlife damages their health, alters natural behaviors, and exposes them to predators and other dangers.
- Protect wildlife and your food by storing rations and trash securely.
- Control pets at all times, or leave them at home.
- Avoid wildlife during sensitive times: mating, nesting, raising young, or winter.

BE CONSIDERATE OF OTHER VISITORS

- Respect other visitors and protect the quality of their experience.
- Be courteous. Yield to other users on the trail.
- Take breaks and camp away from trails and other visitors.
- Let nature's sounds prevail. Avoid loud voices and noises.

Here are a few other principles and policies unique to the Superior Hiking Trail.

FOLLOW THE RULES

- On the SHT, signs may request that you stay on the trail in some areas. It may be an ecologically sensitive area or it may be private land where the owner has specified that hikers stay on the trail as a condition of usage.
- Camp only in official campsites while in state parks (fees required).

TRAVELING

- Select proper footwear. Heavy "waffle stompers" cause much more trail damage than lightweight boots.
- Stay on the trail. Switchbacks and other trail features are there to

prevent erosion and other damage.

• Never blaze trees or leave other markers.

MAKING CAMP

• Use designated campsites only. There are over 70 campsites conveniently located along the SHT.

• Large groups should use sites designated "Multi-group" sites.

• Camping is allowed at designated campsites on a first-come, first-use basis. Be willing to share your campsite.

• Use the tent pad areas that have been cleared and do not trench around the tent.

• Avoid landscaping or otherwise "improving" the campsite other than removing sharp twigs and rocks from under the tent.

• Never cut trees or other vegetation or pound nails into trees.

COOKING

• Try to use a stove rather than a fire. Stoves are easier, cleaner and more reliable.

• It is necessary to boil, filter or chemically treat all water for cooking and drinking.

• Follow all forest fire restrictions. If fires are allowed, use only dead and down wood. Do not peel the bark from birch trees.

CLEAN-UP

• Try cleaning dishes with only hot water and a scrubby.

• Pour all water out on the ground at least 200 feet from any water source.

• Do not wash or bathe in any stream or lake. Wash and rinse at least 200 feet from a water source.

GET TOGETHER AND HELP OUT

• Join the SHTA and help maintain or build the trail.

• Support environmental organizations.

• Organize a group to clean up and/or repair damage in local areas.

The Best of the
Superior Hiking Trail

EVERY SECTION OF THE SUPERIOR HIKING TRAIL is the best...for some reason. Over the years, some sections have become better known than others. People have voted with their feet for favorites like Oberg Mountain in the fall. Here are suggestions for your hiking selection.

CROWD FAVORITES

These sections are scenic and easy to reach. They are popular for good reason. Be prepared for great hiking and a few other folks along the trail.

- Split Rock River loop: Up and down the banks of this spirited river (5.0 miles, see page 70-73).

- Bean and Bear lakes: Climb to a mountainous setting and enjoy the scenic lakes below (3 miles one-way, see page 84-88).

- Mount Trudee: A long gradual uphill to views of Tettegouche lakes (4.8 miles one-way from Tettegouche, see pages 89-91).

- Carlton Peak: A steep climb to the biggest, but not highest mountain in Minnesota (3.1 miles one-way from Temperance River, 1.7 miles one-way from Sawbill Trail, see pages 126-129).

- Oberg Mountain: A great meander to scenic views, especially in fall colors (1.8 mile loop, see page 136).

LOOPS

No need to shuttle or return along the same trail with these routes.

- Caribou River: From trailhead go up one side of the river, cross the bridge beyond the falls, and return on the other side (1.5 miles, see page 114-116).

- Moose Mountain gondola loop: Ride gondola to top of Moose Mountain, then hike back down through maple woods (3.5 miles hiking, see pages 137-139).

- Cascade River: Go up one side of the river to Co. Rd. 45 and return on the other (7.8 miles, see page 151-156).

- Pincushion Mountain: Follow SHT either way around loop trail (4.7 miles, see pages 163-165).

Also note many loop hiking opportunities where SHT enters or leaves state parks, including the Voyageur Trail in Gooseberry State Park, Tettegouche State Park trails along the Baptism River, and the high ridges of Cascade State Park.

LOLLIPOP LOOPS

You'll hike in a bit, then hit a smaller loop.

- Cove Point spur: From Cove Point Lodge up to radio tower, take one fork to main SHT and return on the other fork (5.8 miles, see page 79).

- Bean and Bear lakes: Take Twin Lakes trail from downtown Silver Bay and loop around past scenic views (6.6 miles, see page 85).

BIKE SHUTTLES

If you have just one car but want to hike through a section, bring a bike for the shuttle. Park at the end with the asterisk and you can ride downhill to the start. Of course, that means you'll hike uphill.

- From Gooseberry Falls State Park to Castle Danger.*
- From Beaver Bay to Silver Bay* (ride along Penn Blvd. and Co. Rd. 4).
- From Temperance River State Park to Cook Co. Rd. 1.*
- From Arrowhead Trail to Jackson Lake Rd.*

WILDERNESS TREKS

Long-distance sections with fewer people along the trail.

• Split Rock to Beaver Bay.
• Finland Recreation Area to Crosby-Manitou State Park.
• Crosby-Manitou State Park to Caribou River.
• Cascade River State Park to Bally Creek Rd.
• Jackson Lake Rd. to Border Route Trail.

SCENIC SHORTIES

Shorter walks to scenic spots.

• Wolf Rock from Castle Danger trailhead (0.5 miles one-way, see pages 61–64).
• Highway 1 to Fantasia overlooks (1.2 miles one-way, see pages 92–95).
• Lake Co. Rd. 6 to Section 13 cliffs (1.3 miles one-way, see pages 98–100).
• Cook Co. Rd. 58 to Devil Track River (1 mile one-way, see pages 163–166).
• Kadunce River (0.7 miles one-way, see pages 172–174).
• Lakewalk section (1.6 miles one-way, see page 176).

BEST TROUT FISHING

Cross the river on a scenic bridge and toss a lure.

• Gooseberry River
• Split Rock River
• Manitou River
• Cascade River
• Poplar River

MOST DRAMATIC PEAKS

• Mount Trudee
• Carlton Peak
• Oberg Mountain
• Ridgeline between Arrowhead Trail and Jackson Lake Rd.

Map Legend

Superior Hiking Trail
Spur trails or other trails

Parking areas **P**

Backcountry campsites, SHT ▲

Multi-group campsites, SHT **M**

Major campgrounds, State Park/commercial **C**

Reference points in text ◄

Main road ———————

Other road ....

State Park boundary —·—·—·—·—·

State highway 61

Major county highway ⑦

Forest service, township roads
or other county roads 158 ◇617◇

NORTH is always to the top of the page. The SHT runs primarily in a SW to NE direction with east-west being predominant.

SCALE 1" = 1 MILE
The gridwork visible on the gray base map indicates one-mile square sections.

Knife River to Lake County Road 102

START (END)
Parking area on Scenic Hwy 61

END (START)
Lake Co. Rd. 102 (Hawk Hill Rd.)

LENGTH OF TRAIL SECTION
4.2 miles

SAFETY CONCERNS
• None

ACCESS AND PARKING
Nearest Hwy. 61 milepost: 18.2

Secondary road name and number: Lake Co. Rd. 103

Etc. 0.3 mile to Scenic Hwy. 61. Right to parking lot on west side of Knife River.

ALTERNATE PARKING AREA
Nearest Hwy. 61 milepost: 18

Secondary road name and number: Lake Co. Rd. 102 (Hawk Hill Rd.)

Etc. Parking on left

FACILITIES
No facilities directly at trailhead. Water, bathrooms, groceries, lodging, camping etc. in the town of Knife River.

SYNOPSIS
This section captures the essence of the unique valley of the Knife River. Though one normally thinks of meandering streams in a flat landscape, here the river has etched its bends deeply into the thick deposits of glacial till and postglacial lake clays, until it hit the resistant basalt bedrock. The trail alternates between the tops of high banks with fine vistas through the pines and riverside stretches and fir-shaded terraces.

MILE-BY-MILE DESCRIPTION

0.0 (4.2)
PARKING LOT, KNIFE RIVER VILLAGE

SHT leaves old Hwy. 61 in Knife River village going west along the south bank of the river in river bottom second growth forest, all new since the heyday of the great Alger Smith logging railroad that supplied millions of white pine logs along this route to the dock at the river mouth. As SHT nears the base of First Falls at 0.4 miles it passes a recently constructed fish ladder and observation station, intended to enhance the river's famous steelhead trout spawning migration. SHT then rises to skirt the edge of a fine grove of old white pines on an upper terrace.

0.5 (3.7)
HIGHWAY 61 EXPRESSWAY

SHT crosses Knife River to its north side on the Expressway bridge, and continues upriver. At 0.7 miles it veers away from the river to the north, but there is a spur that continues another 0.4 miles along the north bank. The SHT climbs gently in second growth until it crosses the gravel East Shilhon Rd. (St. Louis Co. Rd. 255, an extension of Lake Co. Rd. 103).

1.1 (3.1)
EAST SHILHON ROAD

SHT rises gently in young fir, birch, and aspen woods. Soon it passes through an open grove of large white pines, and comes to another nice stand of white and red pines that mark the top of the river bank. SHT follows the east bank of the river among red and white pines, cedar and spruce. There is a nice vista upriver between the pines. Eventually SHT descends to a lower river terrace. Note an old copper-prospecting pit and dump on the side of the trail away from the river. Soon the SHT descends to the top of Second Falls, where the river tumbles over large outcrops of old basalt lava flows.

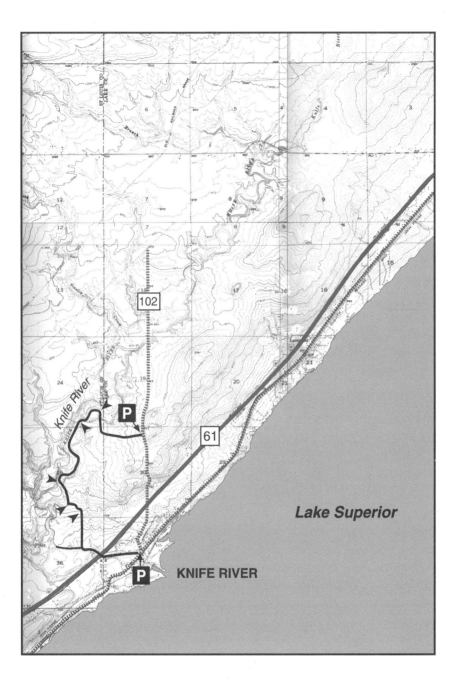

Lake Superior

102

61

KNIFE RIVER

2.1 (2.1)
TOP OF SECOND FALLS

An OHV trail comes in from the east; SHT continues north a few yards in from the river bank on a low terrace in a dark fir forest, climbing steep clay banks briefly before it descends again to the riverside at Cap's Spring and a young black ash grove. At a sharp right bend in the river, a big, old and open-grown white pine commands the opposite bank. SHT turns northeast among some pines and then along an old terrace in dark, thick firs and spruce. Soon two ATV trails cross the SHT, which then gradually rises to a junction overlooking another sharp right bend in the river.

3.1 (1.1)
SPUR TRAIL AT RIVER BEND

A short spur drops to the riverside with its basalt bedrock and white cedars, while the SHT climbs along the top of a high bank, but soon descends to river level again at a sharp riverbend. Across a little ash swamp it soon veers away from the river to the east across a dark, fir-covered terrace. As it approaches the river again it climbs a ridge to the top of another high, slumping bank. SHT climbs away from the river through a mixed forest to Lake Co. Rd. 102.

4.2 (0.0)
LAKE CO. RD. 102 (HAWK HILL RD.)

Two Harbors to Lake County Road 301

START (END)
Superior Shores Resort
parking lot

END (START)
Lake Co. Rd. 301 (Fors Rd.)

LENGTH OF TRAIL SECTIONS
0.9 miles (southwest end) and
2.7 miles (northeast end)

SAFETY CONCERNS
• Crossing Hwy. 61

ACCESS AND PARKING
Nearest Hwy. 61 milepost: 27.2

Parking available in Superior
Shores parking lot. Use northwest
corner of lot (farthest from lodge
and closest to trail).

For parking at the northeast end
see next section.

FACILITIES
At Superior Shores

Designated campsites on this section of SHT: one

SYNOPSIS
Most of this stretch traverses
fairly level lake plain in mixed
second-growth forest, with occasional old pine stumps as hints
of forests past. The main feature
is the 0.7 mile run along the
beautiful little gorge of rocky
and tumbling Silver Creek.

As of Spring 2001, this section
of the SHT is incomplete.

MILE-BY-MILE DESCRIPTION: SOUTHWESTERN END

0.0 (0.9)
SUPERIOR SHORES RESORT

From the northwest corner of the Superior Shores parking lot SHT crosses Hwy. 61, enters a mixed forest and soon crosses an unnamed creek. SHT intersects with the Two Harbors Municipal Ski Trail several times before coming to a dead end. This short hike makes a great leg stretcher for those with just a little time.

MILE-BY-MILE DESCRIPTION: NORTHEASTERN END

0.0 (2.7)
LAKE CO. RD. 301 (FORS RD.)

SHT heads west through generally flat ground in mixed forest, crossing a tributary of Silver Creek. SHT arrives high above Silver Creek and descends a steep slope into the creek valley. SHT follows the creek upstream along the northeast bank to a split log bridge and the entrance to the campsite.

▲ SILVER CREEK CAMPSITE

TYPE: Regular
TENT PADS: 3
WATER: From silver creek
SETTING: Northeast side of silver creek, 1.2 miles west of Co. Rd. 301
PREVIOUS CAMPSITE: None
NEXT CAMPSITE: 8.8 miles to the east

1.2 (1.5)
SILVER CREEK BRIDGE

SHT turns to the left and heads downstream, coming out into the rocky edge of the streambed itself for a few yards. SHT may be water covered during high water times. SHT passes through a grove of tall pines as it wanders along the creek edge or on top of high banks where the creek has undercut the basalt bedrock. SHT suddenly turns right and heads steeply up away from Silver Creek through regenerating aspen to an open area.

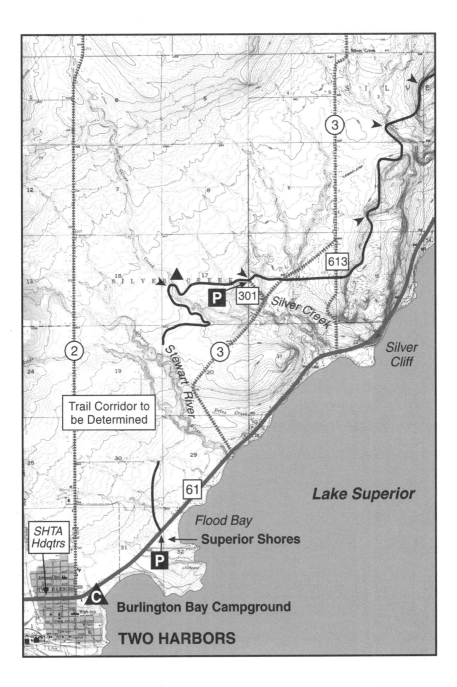

Trail Corridor to be Determined

Lake Superior

Silver Cliff

Silver Creek

SHTA Hdqtrs

Flood Bay

Superior Shores

Burlington Bay Campground

TWO HARBORS

2.2 (0.5)
JUNCTION WITH SNOWMOBILE TRAIL
White posts mark this intersection. SHT jogs right at the first post
then left at the second post. SHT moves through birch-aspen-alder-
black ash woods, passing an occasional red maple to a junction with
another snowmobile trail. Some of this land was a recent clearcut.
Taking a left on the snowmobile trail brings you to the Stewart River.

2.7 (0.0)
END OF TRAIL

Lake County Road 301 to Castle Danger

START (END)
Lake Co. Rd. 301 (Fors Rd.)

END (START)
Silver Creek Township Rd. 617 (West Castle Danger Rd.)

LENGTH OF TRAIL SECTION
6.3 miles

SAFETY CONCERNS
• Some steep walking in Crow Creek ravine

ACCESS AND PARKING
Nearest Hwy. 61 milepost: 28.5

Secondary road name and number: Follow Lake Co. Rd. 3 for 2.0 miles. Turn left on Lake Co. Rd. 301 (Fors Rd.) for 0.3 mile.

Etc: No official parking lot. Park in grassy area near trailhead sign.

FACILITIES
At starting trailhead (farthest southwest): none

Designated campsites on this section of SHT: none

SYNOPSIS
This hike allows you literally to leave civilization behind, as the trail runs from rolling valleys up to rocky, pine-studded ridgelines. The Encampment River is a quietly scenic halfway point, while the stunted trees and expansive views to the east are reminiscent of a hike at timberline in the Rockies. Variety of terrain and forest combine with proximity to towns to make this a good choice for a day hike.

MILE-BY-MILE DESCRIPTION

0.0 (6.3)
LAKE CO. RD. 301 (FORS RD.)

SHT heads easterly in fir-dominated woods, soon descending past big, open-grown spruces to another branch of Silver Creek. It continues east along an old ditch in open woods and an overgrown field, soon coming to Lake Co. Rd. 3, lined with planted jack pines.

0.7 (5.6)
LAKE CO. RD. 3

SHT crosses the highway at an acute angle and soon crosses an ATV trail, then descends steeply to the bridge over Wilson Creek. A few big old yellow birches and a small grove of cedars enhance the creek bottom. SHT then climbs back out to the flat upland at the edge of an old field dotted with young spruces and firs. It temporarily joins an ATV trail at a dip, rising slightly in mixed woods with some ash and balsam poplar in the wetter spots. A few young sugar maples add diversity as SHT approaches Silver Creek Township Rd. 613.

1.1 (5.2)
SILVER CREEK 613 (LOOP RD.)

SHT departs from 613 through a mixed forest of ash, aspen and alder, then climbs gradually, crossing road to radio communication tower, over a rocky ridge and down through thick balsam, crossing the old Beaver Bay Rd. bed and a creek before a steep climb.

2.3 (4.0)
SCRAGGLY OVERLOOK

Views of the Two Harbors area to the west from a ridge of red pines and spruce. SHT then passes through private land, running due north-south and due east-west through white pine and cedar. Hikers are asked to be respectful of owner's rights and stay on the SHT. No camping or fires on private land.

3.6 (2.7)
ENCAMPMENT RIVER CROSSING

SHT descends to the bridge crossing, then climbs to top of ridge east of the Encampment River, then continues along a ridgeline, with views

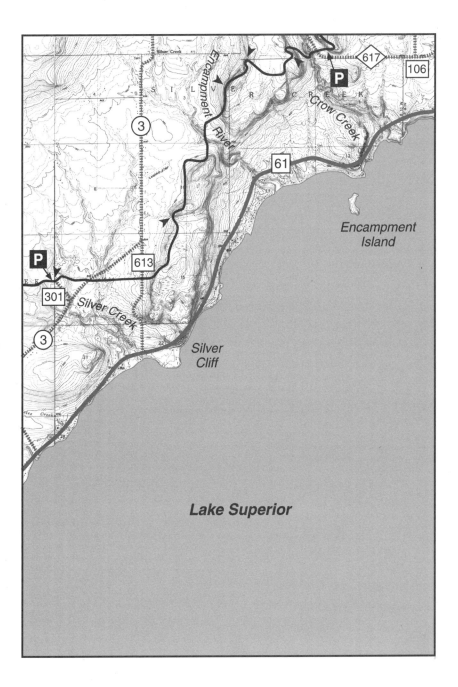

of the Silver Creek, Stewart and Encampment River valleys, a relatively lush agricultural setting. The dwarfed spruces and pines and the mossy ground combine with the wide view to give this section the feel of hiking at timberline in high mountains.

4.3 (2.0)
RED PINE OVERLOOK

Wide view from a red-pine framed outcrop into valley below before SHT turns into the forest and down into a low, wet area. SHT continues into a mixed maple forest. A scenic view (with a bench) across the Crow Creek valley includes pine-studded Wolf Rock. This is private land, so please respect the owner's rights. Wooden steps lead steeply into the river gorge. Note the visible flows of rock in the cliffs of the creek. A 40-foot footbridge crosses Crow Creek, then SHT climbs a talus slope. Watch for "Poison Ivy" sign along the slope. This is the only place along SHT where poison ivy may be found. SHT continues through birches, across Silver Creek Township Rd. 617, then skirts , base of Wolf Rock's dramatic cliffs into parking lot.

6.3 (0.0)
SILVER CREEK TOWNSHIP RD. 617
(WEST CASTLE DANGER RD.) PARKING LOT

Castle Danger to Gooseberry Falls State Park

START (END)
Silver Creek Township Rd. 617 (West Castle Danger Rd.), north of Castle Danger

END (START)
Gooseberry Falls State Park interpretive center

LENGTH OF TRAIL SECTION
8.6 miles

SAFETY CONCERNS
- Rocky cliffs at Wolf Rock— keep children in hand

- Hunting along SHT—wear bright clothing in deer season

- Changing course of meandering Gooseberry River

ACCESS AND PARKING
Nearest Hwy. 61 milepost: 36.6. Intersection marked by SHTA sign.

Secondary road name and number: Lake Co. Rd. 106 (West Castle Danger Rd.), which becomes Silver Creek Township Rd. 617 after 0.6 miles.

Etc: Go 2.4 miles on Lake Co. Rd. 106/Silver Creek Township Rd. 617. Lot is on right.

Parking spaces available: Approximately 6 spaces at Silver Creek Township Rd. 617 parking lot. Overnight okay.

FACILITIES
At starting trailhead (farthest southwest): none

Designated campsites on this section of SHT: four

SYNOPSIS
This section of the SHT has four distinct variations: the ridge between Wolf Rock and Mike's Rock, the low ground to the Gooseberry River, along the river, and in the state park. The two miles along the river outside the park are particularly charming, with beautiful fall colors, migrating waterfowl in season and great agate beaches.

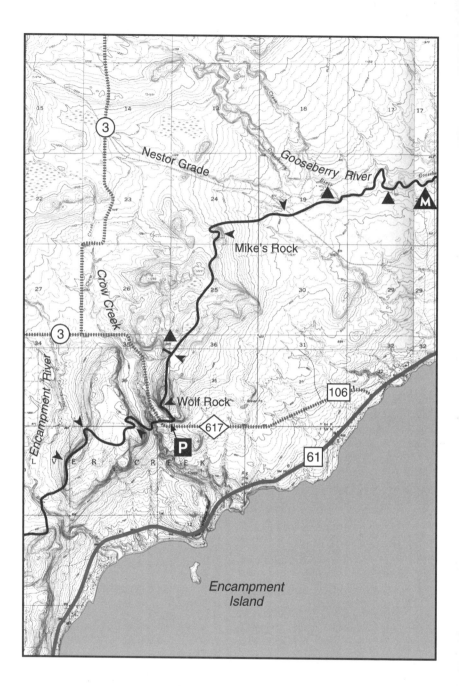

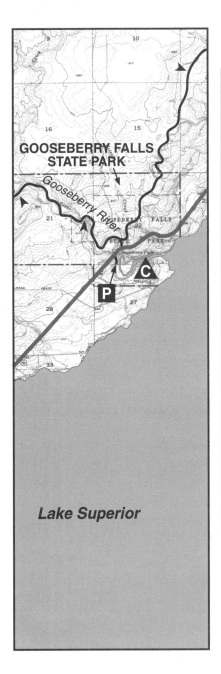

GOOSEBERRY FALLS
STATE PARK

Gooseberry River

GOOSEBERRY FALLS
STATE PARK

P **C**

Lake Superior

BERRIES OF THE
SUPERIOR HIKING TRAIL

Many hikers indulge in the satisfying experience of eating as they hike along the Superior Hiking Trail. Several species of berries are common along the trail, and they ripen from July to September. Blueberries are frequent on the rocky outcrops and scenic overlooks. These, as well as other sweet fruit species, need the full sun that is available on the hill crests. But don't limit your foraging to blueberries; keep your eyes peeled for strawberries, raspberries, thimbleberries, and juneberries. Bring along a bag or bucket—and remember, some berries are poisonous so eat only fruit that you know.

MILE-BY-MILE DESCRIPTION

0.0 (8.6)
SILVER CREEK 617 PARKING LOT

SHT departs right side of parking lot, winds up through cliffs to the top of Wolf Rock. This may be one of the most dramatic first half-miles of the SHT as the SHT winds up to top of Wolf Rock with its pine-clad rock outcrops.

0.5 (8.1)
WOLF ROCK

Great views at 1200' of the Lake, Crow Creek valley, white pine, etc. Note: SHT passes through a mile of private land. Hikers are asked to be respectful and stay on the SHT. No camping or fires on private land. SHT turns away from the valley as the woods alternate from open understory to dense growth. Lots of dead birch in this section, plus large mammal signs. Decomposed lava looks like gravel on the trailbed. SHT is wide with some mud holes when wet.

1.1 (7.5)
SIDE TRAIL TO VISTA

215 yards to vista overlooking Crow Creek valley. SHT continues along ridge, departing private land, through a cedar grove which is the source of a stream, and up and down some rocky spots. The woods alternate from open understory to a dense growth enclosing the SHT in a "green tunnel."

▲ CROW CREEK VALLEY CAMPSITE

TYPE: Regular
TENT PADS: 3
WATER: From small stream
SETTING: 1.3 miles north of Silver Creek 617
PREVIOUS CAMPSITE: 8.8 miles
NEXT CAMPSITE: 3.4 miles

2.9 (5.7)
MIKE'S ROCK

Vistas north and east to Gooseberry River Valley and Lake. SHT descends with stone steps past outcrops to low area of open birch and maple, crosses small stream and marshy area. Some dead birch in here, due to cumulative stress of recent years of drought, damage by birch leaf miner beetle and tent caterpillars.

4.0 (4.6)
NESTOR GRADE
This is an old logging railroad that was used for transporting logs to the Lake, and used now by ATVs. SHT climbs to higher, drier ground and a beautiful stand of birch trees. Berry bushes abundant, including raspberry and thimbleberry. SHT crosses several intermittent streams and reaches overlook on low area. Lots of beaver signs, including two very large beaver dams.

4.6 (4.0)
GOOSEBERRY RIVER AND CAMPSITE
Note gravel meander bars along river—this is a good source of agates. SHT continues along river, an unusual setting due to meanders and oxbow cutoffs. SHT subject to flooding as it alternates from flood plain to berm. These two miles of the SHT have no particular landmark, though look for an old fisherman's cabin at 6.0 (2.6) miles. This section is particularly beautiful in the fall and early spring. Many paths where beaver drag branches to water. Also, watch for migrating waterfowl in spring and fall.

▲ **WEST GOOSEBERRY CAMPSITE**

TYPE: Regular
TENT PADS: 4
WATER: From Gooseberry River
SETTING: 3.9 miles from Gooseberry Falls, on a hill
PREVIOUS CAMPSITE: 3.4 miles
NEXT CAMPSITE: 0.9 mile

▲ **EAST GOOSEBERRY CAMPSITE**

TYPE: Regular
TENT PADS: 4
WATER: From Gooseberry River
SETTING: 3.0 miles from Gooseberry Falls, on a small knoll
PREVIOUS CAMPSITE: 0.9 mile
NEXT CAMPSITE: 0.8 mile

GOOSEBERRY FALLS STATE PARK

Rocky Lake Superior shoreline and five waterfalls highlight Gooseberry Falls State Park. The park was established in 1933, and the Civilian Conservation Corps developed the park between 1934 and 1941, including the stone buildings, campground, picnic area, and trails. These structures have earned Gooseberry Falls State Park a place on the National Register of Historic Places. Today the park covers 1662 acres and includes a 70-site drive-in campground, a rustic group camp at the former CCC camp location, and 18 miles of hiking trails (including a self-guided trail along the Gooseberry River). The visitor center and wayside rest off of Highway 61 serves as an interpretive center and nature store. Its selection of quality outdoor education material is unsurpassed in the area. Interpretive programs are provided during the summer and include guided walks, activities, and evening programs.

▲ GOOSEBERRY RIVER MULTI-GROUP CAMPSITE

TYPE: Multi-group
TENT PADS: 8
WATER: From Gooseberry River
SETTING: 2.2 miles from
   Gooseberry Falls trailhead,
   30 yards off of river
PREVIOUS CAMPSITE: 0.8 mile
NEXT CAMPSITE: 5.3 miles (or
   use Gooseberry Falls State
   Park)

6.7 (1.9)
JUNCTION WITH PARK TRAIL

Wide, grassy trail follows river for a distance, past shelter and up the hill. Trail junction has arrows and "You are here" sign. Pass 10' fence which protects young trees from deer damage, called a "deer excloser." Trail turns left to river and Fifth Falls.

7.8 (0.8)
FIFTH FALLS BRIDGE

After crossing river SHT follows park's Voyageur Trail along east side of Gooseberry River, past gorgeous Fifth Falls.

8.4 (0.2)
JUNCTION WITH SPUR TRAIL

For through hikers, SHT turns sharply to the left at the old Visitors Center (stone building) and heads northeast to Split Rock River. The spur trail to the trailhead turns right and follows paved path to the highway bridge and then under the bridge to the Gooseberry Falls State Park Visitors Center.

8.6 (0.0)
GOOSEBERRY FALLS STATE PARK VISITORS CENTER

Gooseberry Falls State Park to Split Rock River

START (END)
Gooseberry Falls State Park
Visitors Center

END (START)
Split Rock River Wayside on
Hwy. 61

LENGTH OF TRAIL SECTION
6.0 miles

SAFETY CONCERNS
• Unreliable water at campsite

ACCESS AND PARKING
Nearest Hwy. 61 milepost: 38.9

Secondary road name and number: none

Etc: Park at Gooseberry Falls
State Park Visitors Center.
Plenty of parking available.
No overnight parking at wayside
area. Overnight parking available
with park sticker. Check in at
Visitors Center.

FACILITIES
At starting trailhead (farthest
southwest): bathrooms, snacks,
telephone, drinking water

Designated campsites on this section of trail: one

SYNOPSIS
Trail starts out at a gentle climb
through many birch, cedar, to
higher elevation with lots of up
and down, crossing bridges, past
campsite to overlook with great
views of Lake Superior including
South and North Shores. Down
to Split Rock River, along river
to wayside.

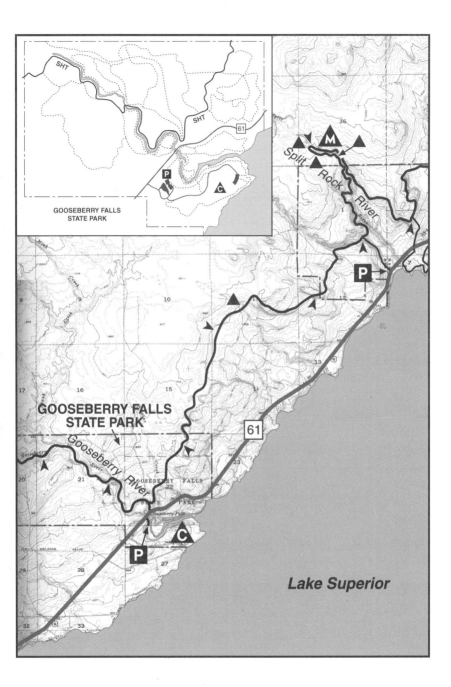

GOOSEBERRY FALLS
STATE PARK

GOOSEBERRY FALLS
STATE PARK

Lake Superior

MILE-BY-MILE DESCRIPTION

0.0 (6.0)
GOOSEBERRY FALLS STATE PARK VISITORS CENTER

Spur trail follows state park ski trails under Hwy. 61 bridge across the Gooseberry River and past the old visitors center, where it intersects main SHT, then through birch and pine, up a high rise and across Nelson's Creek. SHT climbs easily to park boundary, along 8-foot wide trail. Well marked at junctions with ski trails. SHT goes under a cedar arch and through a cedar grove, onto private land.

1.2 (4.8)
SHT SIGN

SHT goes through aspen, birch, and dogwood, follows park boundary signs, then crosses onto private land (as marked by sign) and a gentle downhill through aspen and cedar, then levels out in a cedar grove. Sign notes contribution of Philip Economon family. SHT follows base of rise on right, then crosses the Fire Mountain trail and five small footbridges across creeks. SHT departs private land and enters a stand of white pines.

PUBLIC-PRIVATE COOPERATION

We take things for granted sometimes—like a clearly marked trail, or a footbridge over a low wet area. In fact, some things we almost can't help but take for granted because we never learn about them. For example, private landowners have helped make the Superior Hiking Trail a reality by sharing their property. More than 10% of the trail crosses land that is privately owned. Less than 1% crosses property of the Superior Hiking Trail Association. As you hike the trail, please remember that you are often a guest!

2.8 (3.2)
BLUEBERRY HILL RD.

SHT crosses dirt road, goes through birch and poplar, across gravel logging road, across split log footbridge, then climbs small hill to cedar grove and past campsite. SHT goes through birch and pine and across small footbridge to an open area which is rocky and mossy, with good views of Lake—perfect for breakfast after staying at campsite, or to

MILE-BY-MILE DESCRIPTION

0.0 (11.3)
TRAILHEAD ON EAST SIDE OF SPLIT ROCK RIVER, ON HWY. 61

Spur trail climbs up wide state park XC trails to junction marked with sign.

0.5 (10.8)
JUNCTION WITH SHT

Turn right to head towards Beaver Bay, left for the loop described above. SHT follows ridgeline, passing two good vistas of Lake and lighthouse, then descends. Some of the rock outcrops are old shore-lines of Glacial Lake Duluth. The long gentle descent leads to a low, boggy area, then the junction with a ski trail, then a wide ski trail bridge over the Little Split Rock River.

1.7 (9.6)
JUNCTION WITH SPUR TO STATE PARK CAMPGROUND

Soon after crossing creek, spur 1.4 miles from state park campground joins SHT. SHT soon joins old Merrill Grade railroad route. SHT follows moss-covered remains of old railroad ties through birch, aspen, and balsam. Watch for sign where SHT departs grade. SHT climbs to long walk along exposed rock ridge with spruce everywhere and rocks and moss on the surface and drop-offs to north. SHT crosses ATV trail at 3.0 miles. Large pines between SHT and view of Lake.

3.4 (7.9)
CHAPINS RIDGE CAMPSITE

Just east of campsite SHT follows 30-foot wooden stairway and crosses stream on split log bridge. SHT crosses logging road, then climbs to overlook atop Christmas Tree Ridge through open grassy area. Good views inland. SHT continues in open area, through a fine stand of white pines, and descends from ridge through brush and aspen, and past a pond.

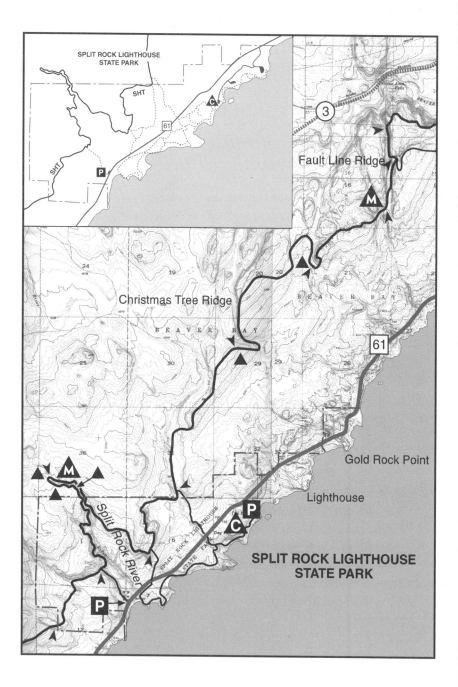

BEAVER BAY

Cove Point

Lake Superior

Established as a park in 1971, today Split Rock Lighthouse State Park includes 1872 acres along Lake Superior between the Split Rock River and the lighthouse. The park hosts a number of historic sites including a commercial fishing village site, an early mine site, the site of a logging camp and dam, and of course the lighthouse and surrounding buildings. One of the unique aspects of the park is the cart-in campground. Campers cart in rather than drive in to the 20 sites located along Lake Superior. Four lakeside backpack sites are also available. Twelve miles of trails connect and follow the lakeshore and the ridge 600 feet above. Another popular pastime, fishing, especially for trout and salmon, is excellent along the Split Rock River.

▲ CHAPINS RIDGE CAMPSITE

TYPE: Regular
TENT PADS: 4
WATER: 0.2 mile away at
    Chapins Creek
SETTING: 1.5 miles east of Merrill
    Grade
PREVIOUS CAMPSITE: 4.7 miles
NEXT CAMPSITE: 2.2 miles

▲ BEAVER POND CAMPSITE

TYPE: regular
TENT PADS: 4
WATER: From beaver pond—treat
    before using
SETTING: 2.0 miles east of
    Chapins Creek
PREVIOUS CAMPSITE: 2.2 miles
NEXT CAMPSITE: 1.5 miles

7.6 (3.7)
BEAVER POND CAMPSITE

SHT passes large beaver pond, old logging camp, then climbs sharply to vistas of north and west. SHT follows rock promontories in a series of short ascents and descents. From ridge SHT descends steeply into valley and wet area. SHT crosses Fault Creek on split-log bridge, passes high mound of giant boulders, then traverses the rocky shore of a beaver pond. SHT climbs steeply through birch forest to Fault Line Ridge, formed by a geologic fault. SHT proceeds along east rim of fault valley, with dramatic views into a deep valley.

HISTORY OF
SPLIT ROCK LIGHTHOUSE

For a few centuries now, people have been trying to move safely along the North Shore of Lake Superior. The Superior Hiking Trail represents one of the first times people have tried to make it harder to get from Duluth to Grand Portage. Split Rock Lighthouse, which is visible from a number of points along the SHT, was one of many efforts to make the trip easier. Built in response to a particularly tragic year of shipwrecks (1905, with 215 lives lost on the Lake), the lighthouse operated from 1910 to 1961. The light was visible up to 60 miles away. Today, the lighthouse is owned by the State of Minnesota and is one of the most popular tourist sites on the North Shore, with over 200,000 visitors a year.

▲ FAULT LINE CREEK CAMPSITE

TYPE: Multi-group
TENT PADS: 8
WATER: From beaver pond—treat before using
SETTING: 3.7 miles from Beaver Bay trailhead, on shore of
    large beaver pond by old logging camp
PREVIOUS CAMPSITE: 1.5 miles
NEXT CAMPSITE: 4.6 miles

8.2 (3.1)
JUNCTION WITH WEST
COVE POINT SPUR

At a major break in Fault Line Ridge, this spur trail leads to Cove Point on the shore (see sidebar). SHT continues along ridgeline, then after one last overlook turns east and follows cliffs above Beaver River. Views include the railroad tracks linking the taconite mines of Babbitt with the processing plant in Silver Bay. Hikers can hear, and in season see, Glen Avon Falls on the Beaver River.

10.0 (1.3)
JUNCTION WITH EAST
COVE POINT SPUR

Take this spur 200 yards to view of Lake or all the way down to the shore. SHT descends towards Co. Rd. 4 through birch, maple, and balsam forests, with groves of cedar in some low areas. SHT crosses a snowmobile trail, which leads 1 mile into Beaver Bay 30 yards before road.

11.3 (0.0)
CO. RD. 4 PARKING LOT

COVE POINT SPUR TRAIL LOOP

This loop section was built in 1996 with assistance from volunteers provided by Cove Point Lodge. With a little less than three new miles of trail a great six-mile loop was created, including the dramatic cliffs above the Beaver River and at the Fault Line Ridge.

The SHT spur begins just above the Cove Point Lodge parking lot, crosses Highway 61 right away and continues upstream, crossing a stream and passing through a former mink farm. After passing a communications tower, at 1.2 miles in comes the junction of the east and west spurs.

The eastern spur leads about a half mile through birch forest to two hills, the second with a dramatic overlook of the Lake and the interior. This was previously a dead end overlook of the original SHT. The eastern spur joins the main SHT 1.8 miles northeast of the western spur. This section of the SHT passes the Beaver River overlook cliffs and the Fault Line Ridge overlooks with their numerous red pines.

The western spur is longer, 1.1 miles. It heads back to Cove Point from the SHT at a major break in the Fault Line Ridge. The western spur ascends a steep rocky staircase, then follows the rim of a gorge to the left. Several small rises are encountered. After crossing and following a stream the western spur meets the eastern spur. The loop is completed.

Beaver Bay to Silver Bay

START (END)
Lake Co. Rd. 4 (Lax Lake Rd.),
0.8 miles north of Beaver Bay

END (START)
Lake Co. Rd. 5 (Penn Blvd.),
north of Silver Bay

LENGTH OF TRAIL SECTION
4.7 miles

SAFETY CONCERNS
• Crossing of active Northshore Mining Company railroad tracks

• Watch trail signs closely as numerous other trails and roads intersect with SHT

ACCESS AND PARKING
Nearest Hwy. 61 milepost: 51.1

Secondary road name and number: 0.7 miles north on Co. Rd. 4

Etc: 6 spaces in lot off Co. Rd. 4. Overnight okay

FACILITIES
At starting trailhead (farthest southwest): outhouses at Beaver River

Designated campsites on this section of SHT: one

SYNOPSIS
The Superior Hiking Trail traces a serpentine route through one of the more developed sections of the North Shore, almost entirely within Silver Bay city limits. Despite the near-constant presence of taconite operations, highways, and towns, this section offers dramatic views as well as an intimate look at the Beaver River and its gorgeous falls. Easy access at both ends makes this a worthwhile journey, especially for the local history buff.

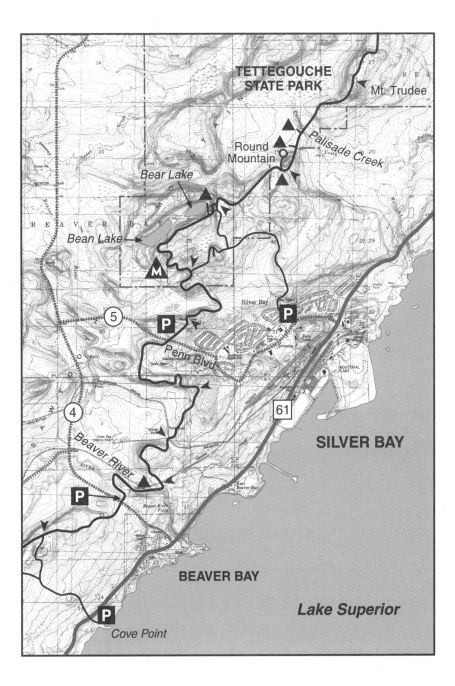

MILE-BY-MILE DESCRIPTION

0.0 (4.7)
LAKE CO. RD. 4 PARKING LOT

SHT leaves lot along snowmobile trail (the Silver Bay Grant-in-Aid Trail) with wide views of valley, tracing beneath some settling ponds, and soon crosses Beaver River on a bridge shared by the SHT and snowmobiles. SHT turns down east bank of river immediately after bridge. This is a scenic river walk past groves of cedar and white pine, following the river as it changes from a gentle wide river to a roaring cascade. Near falls, SHT turns away from river and climbs through cedar, spruce, and birch to join the Betzler Rd. SHT turns left or north on the road. Arrow may be missing or inaccurate here.

▲ BEAVER RIVER CAMPSITE

TYPE: Regular
TENT PADS: 3
WATER: From Beaver River*
SETTING: 1.0 mile east of Beaver
   Bay trailhead
PREVIOUS CAMPSITE: 4.6 miles
NEXT CAMPSITE: 5.8 miles

*Because of taconite tailings
pipeline spill in fall 2000, water may
still be impotable. Check with DNR
before drinking. Regular
filters won't filter out tailings.

MINNESOTA'S TACONITE INDUSTRY

Since the 1950s, the history and landscape of the Beaver Bay area have been tied to the processing and shipping of taconite, a low-grade iron ore found naturally in deposits 50 miles inland. Reserve Mining Company built the world's first large taconite concentrating and pelletizing plant, creating the company town of Silver Bay.

In the 1970s Reserve Mining drew criticism for its practice of dumping many thousands of tons of taconite tailings into Lake Superior daily. Following a 1978 federal court ruling, Reserve built the immense Milepost 7 tailings pond a few miles behind Beaver Bay. The tailings sludge is pumped through huge pipes from the Silver Bay plant. Reserve Mining Co. closed its Babbitt mine and Silver Bay plant in 1986. In 1989, Cyprus Minerals Company bought the plant and reopened it on a smaller scale.

1.1 (3.6)
RAILROAD TRACKS CROSSING
This is the main line bringing taconite to Cyprus Northshore for processing from a mine in Babbitt. SHT follows Betzler Rd. for another 100 yards, then at major intersection goes due north into a balsam thicket, then up a nice, fragrant stand of red and white pines to Sulheim's Overlook, a rocky knob with a partial 360° view of ridges, rivers, Silver Bay Golf Course, and taconite operations. SHT continues along cliff edge with views of tailings ponds and the pumping station below.

2.2 (2.5)
GOLF COURSE RD. CROSSING
SHT crosses a jumble of roads, a snowmobile trail, and the double-barreled pipeline of the famous Milepost 7 operation. SHT picks up again in a grove of young aspens, immediately recrosses a newer dirt road, then leads gradually uphill to an overlook amidst red pines with views of Lake. This is the most remote feeling part of this section of the SHT, with little sense of the development around. As visible from the overlook, the forest here is a sea of birches with occasional towering white and red pines. SHT continues through this forest, up a ridgeline, across an ATV trail and then up to a rocky open ridgeline.

3.2 (1.5)
VIEW OF SILVER BAY, NORTHSHORE MINING PLANT
SHT follows ridge overlooking Silver Bay, taconite operations, Beaver River valley, Palisade Head, etc. Note unusual clumps of low, leafy bearberry and juniper. SHT winds along first ridge, past a spur to the nearby residential neighborhood of Silver Bay, then descends and climbs again to a second ridge, called "Blueberry Ridge" by the locals. SHT follows the Beaver River side of the ridge. From a clump of red pines one can look back to the parking lot on Co. Rd. 4 where the hike began. A beaver pond below provides an opportunity for watching the busy ones at work. SHT descends into mixed woods, past a trail, through a wet area with ash trees, then gently up to one final rocky ridge before swinging down past a snowmobile trail to Penn Blvd.

4.7 (0.0)
PENN BLVD.
Parking available here. SHT continues on other side of Penn.

Silver Bay to Tettegouche State Park and Highway 1

START (END)
Lake Co. Rd. 5 (Penn Blvd.),
north of Silver Bay

END (START)
State Hwy. 1 (or Tettegouche
State Park Trail Center)

LENGTH OF TRAIL SECTION
11.1 miles

SAFETY CONCERNS
• Trail often follows cliff edges,
so use caution with small children. Steep downhills can be
slippery in wet weather.

ACCESS AND PARKING
Nearest Hwy. 61 milepost: 54.3
(stoplight at Outer Drive)

Secondary road name and number: Outer Drive, take through
town to the stop sign at which
point the road becomes Lake Co.
Rd. 5 (same as Penn Blvd.) and
proceed 0.5 mile to roadside
parking at signed SHT crossing.
Plenty of parking in lot.
Overnight okay.

TWIN LAKES TRAIL
Take Outer Drive 0.5 miles from
Hwy. 61 to Bay Area Historical

Society parking lot on right.
SHT spur leaves from far end of
lot. Spur is also labelled "Twin
Lakes Trail" (for Bean and Bear
Lakes). Plenty of parking.
Overnight okay with permission
from Historical Society.

FACILITIES
At starting trailhead (farthest
southwest): none

Designated campsites on this section of SHT: five

SYNOPSIS
This is one of the more challenging sections of the SHT, with
lots of up and down, great views
of the Lake and inland bluffs. It
begins in the outskirts of Silver
Bay and winds past beautiful
Bean and Bear Lakes into
Tettegouche State Park. The
thick maple forests make it a
popular fall colors hike.

MILE-BY-MILE DESCRIPTION

0.0 (11.1)
PENN BLVD.

SHT departs parking area up rock stairway, crosses an ATV trail, past a sumac stand, across a gravel road (to Silver Bay's water supply), and then passes under a powerline into spruces. SHT then ascends ridgeline and crosses another ATV trail.

1.0 (10.1)
SERIES OF OUTCROPS WITH SOUTH AND WEST VIEWS

Views over Silver Bay, water tower, Northshore Mining plant, and Lake. View at 1.3 miles of oak-maple-birch ridge. SHT climbs rock stairs. Green or blue paint on rocks marks SHT route, although these are not official markers.

1.8 (9.3)
WESTERN JUNCTION WITH TWIN LAKES TRAIL

One of two junctions with the Twin Lakes Trail, also makes for a nice "lollipop loop" hike through maples. SHT crosses footbridge on Penn Creek, enters forest with maples dominating the low portion of the south-facing slope, then passes outcrops with oak and sumac. Lots of blueberries and juneberries in

TWIN LAKES TRAIL

How about a walk through town? When the town is nestled in the wilderness like Silver Bay, that can be quite a trek. The Twin Lakes Trail, named after the dramatic Bean and Bear Lakes, is a 6.6 mile "lollipop loop" that has a "stem" of 2.3 miles before it splits apart to visit the lakes.

The trail starts at the Bay Area Historical Society parking lot in Silver Bay. Watch for the distinctive Twin Lakes Trail signs. It crosses Banks Blvd., then continues up a hill and a very nice little hogback area. After 0.7 mile watch for a spur trail on the right; it's 0.7 miles long with some nice views of the City. You'll find interesting views looking west. After crossing ATV trails, at 2.3 miles is the loop junction.

The 0.7 mile west spur leads to Elam's Knob, a lovely spot for a break, about halfway along this side plus a short climb. The east spur takes you up a rocky hillside.

The 1.6 miles of the SHT this loop contains are among the most picturesque of the whole trail. At the end, head over to the Dairy Queen. This may be one of the most scenic hikes anywhere you can end with a Peanut Buster Parfait!

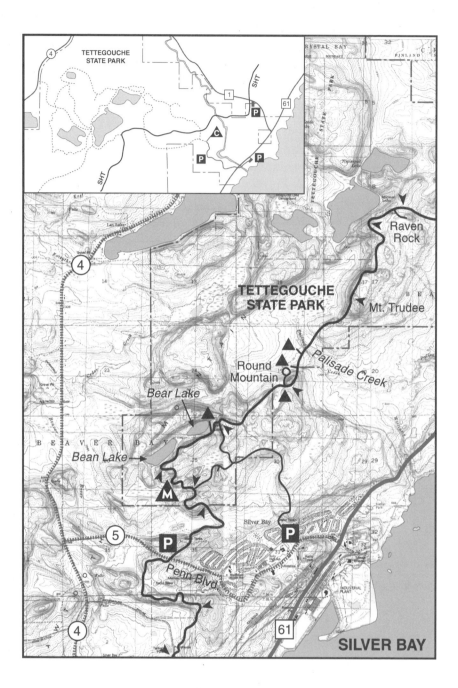

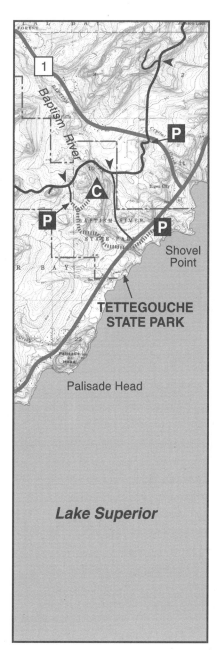

Lake Superior

Palisade Head

TETTEGOUCHE STATE PARK

Shovel Point

this part of the SHT. At one outcrop you can see back to the previous outcrop, and a beaver pond before SHT descends.

⚠ PENN CREEK CAMPSITE

TYPE: Multi-group
TENT PADS: 8
WATER: From Penn Creek
SETTING: 2.0 miles east of
   Penn Blvd.
PREVIOUS CAMPSITE: 5.8 miles
NEXT CAMPSITE: 1.4 miles

2.6 (8.5)
BEAN LAKE OVERLOOK

From overlook Mt. Trudee is visible to the east, marked by dark red pines and a flat top. SHT passes overlooks on Silver Bay, Milepost 7, and beaver ponds, but mostly looks down on Bean and Bear Lakes. The Bean Lake overlook is impressive, with an open platform of rock hundreds of feet directly above the lake. SHT also passes the remains of a log cabin, built by local children in the 1950's. Watch for spur to Bear Lake campsite at 3.4 (7.7).

▲ BEAR LAKE CAMPSITE

TYPE: Regular
TENT PADS: 4
WATER: From Bear Lake
SETTING: 3.4 miles east of Penn Blvd., 150 yards off SHT on spur,
   on NE corner of Bear Lake
PREVIOUS CAMPSITE: 1.4 miles
NEXT CAMPSITE: 1.2 miles

3.6 (7.5)
EASTERN JUNCTION WITH TWIN LAKES TRAIL

At top of bluff, find the next junction with Twin Lakes Trail. Head 0.1 mile left for an excellent view of both Bean and Bear Lakes, then cross a snowmobile trail to Silver Bay (4.0/7.1). SHT goes through level maple-birch woods, drops to an overlook of valley and view of Round Mtn. and Mt. Trudee. SHT descends to Beaver Pond.

▲ ROUND MOUNTAIN BEAVER POND CAMPSITE

TYPE: Regular
TENT PADS: 6
WATER: From beaver pond—treat before using
SETTING: 0.1 mile west of Round Mountain spur
PREVIOUS CAMPSITE: 1.2 miles
NEXT CAMPSITE: 0.8 mile

4.8 (6.3)
SPUR TRAIL UP ROUND MTN.

1/4-mile trail to dramatic overlook on the expansive Palisade Creek Valley. SHT passes mature sugar maple forest and descends into Palisade Creek Valley, crossing ATV trail, two split-log foot bridges and a wet area with white cedars. SHT crosses West Palisade Creek. 300-yard spur trail to campsite. SHT then passes East Palisade Creek campsite and descends to 25' bridge over East Palisade Creek. Good water source (treat before drinking). SHT crosses ATV trail, climbs past a series of wooden steps through mixed woods to Lake and valley view.

▲ WEST PALISADE CREEK CAMPSITE

TYPE: Regular
TENT PADS: 5
WATER: From West Palisade Creek
SETTING: 1.0 mile west of Mt. Trudee
PREVIOUS CAMPSITE: 0.8 mile
NEXT CAMPSITE: 0.2 mile

▲ EAST PALISADE CREEK CAMPSITE

TYPE: Regular
TENT PADS: 4
WATER: From East Palisade Creek
SETTING: 0.8 miles west of Mt. Trudee
PREVIOUS CAMPSITE: 0.2 mile
NEXT CAMPSITE: 7.8 miles
(or use Tettegouche State Park)

6.3 (4.8)
MT. TRUDEE

Mt. Trudee offers one of the SHT's best examples of a large, weather-resistant anorthosite dome. Its summit is picturesque, studded with pines. View north to 3 lakes, south over Lake, Tettegouche State Park headquarters. SHT continues along top of Trudee, with views including Tettegouche and Micmac Lakes (named after lakes in Labrador, Canada), then descends through almost pure sugar maple forest. Forest changes to mixed maple-birch, starting at a series of rock walls alongside SHT. There is a short spur to a view of Mt. Trudee and the Palisade Valley. This was the area proposed by Reserve Mining to fill with taconite tailings.

TETTEGOUCHE STATE PARK

Tettegouche State Park was established in 1979, and contains over 9000 acres of land, including six inland lakes and one mile of Lake Superior shoreline. Flowing through the park is the Baptism River and on it, High Falls, the highest falls completely in Minnesota. At the southeast corner of the park lies Palisade Head, a high bluff with a sheer rock face falling 200 feet into Lake Superior below. The park has 34 semi-modern campsites. The rugged, semi-mountainous terrain, and spectacular overlooks, make hiking on the park's seventeen miles of trails very popular. A one-mile self-guided trail to Shovel Point along Lake Superior educates as well as inspires. For the history buff, there is the Tettegouche Camp, a 1910 social camp. Its log buildings have been restored for group rentals. In addition, there is rich logging, maple syruping, and mining history throughout the park.

WOLF RIDGE ENVIRONMENTAL LEARNING CENTER

The Wolf Ridge Environmental Learning Center (WRELC) facility is a cluster of buildings with 1000 acres of surrounding land which accommodates hundreds of students, both youth and adult. Wolf Ridge has been at its current site since 1988, though the program started in Isabella, Minnesota, in the early 1970s. The well-regarded residential environmental education program has introduced over a quarter-million students to the wonders of the north woods; weekend programs offer a wide variety of experiences for adults and families. The trails on the WRELC intersect with the SHT, allowing for excursions onto the SHT from the WRELC parking lot. Look for its marked turnoff a few miles up Lake Co. Rd. 6.

7.5 (3.6)
JUNCTION WITH STATE PARK TRAIL

Park post with letter "L." State park trail goes 1.0 mile to Tettegouche Camp and Conservancy Pines. SHT continues on state park trail, first through pure maples, past mileage sign, and over a 40-foot plank bridge, then through low area and a copse of white cedars. A spur trail leads to good views from Raven Rock.

8.2 (2.9)
JUNCTION WITH STATE PARK TRAIL

Park post with letter "C." Tricky spot on maps. SHT descends through mixed maple-birch-conifer forest, past a 12' circumference white pine, then through "The Drainpipe," a 150' rock crevice with rock steps. SHT emerges into dominant birch stand being replaced by the spruce and balsam fir understory. SHT crosses another ski trail and leads through white cedar lowland. Look for spur trail up to view of Lake, Palisade Head, etc.

9.7 (1.4)
JUNCTION WITH ACCESS TRAIL TO TETTEGOUCHE STATE PARK TRAILHEAD PARKING LOT

Park post with letter "B." To access Tettegouche parking lot, turn on ski trail. 0.3 mile downhill to parking lot, through a white pine grove, passing state park post "A." Straight on SHT through mature birch, across plank walkways. Watch for spur trail to state park campground.

SHT descends wooden stairs past Baptism High Falls overlook, then crosses Baptism River on suspension bridge just above the falls. These are the highest falls entirely in Minnesota. The bridge, built in 1991 with substantial help from Minnesota Power, has a unique single-cable suspension design. This was by far the most elaborate and expensive bridge built by the SHTA. At trailside bench, look for spur trail to base of High Falls. SHT leaves river and goes up wood staircase.

10.4 (0.7)
JUNCTION WITH STATE PARK TRAIL

Side trail follows river downstream 1.3 miles to park headquarters. SHT goes into birch woods and across a narrow roadbed. Two large white pines on the side, followed by a balsam fir "tunnel" for 200 yards. SHT leads through cedars, up a hill and along a ridge, then climbs 100-yard staircase. The large rock amphitheater is a former quarry site, the first quarry used in the first days of the 3M Company. Spur leads to SHT parking lot off Hwy. 1.

11.1 (0.0)
STATE HWY. 1

SUGAR MAPLE FORESTS

The extensive maple forests of the SHT, which create much of the gorgeous colors of a fall hike, are the result of a lucky combination of ecological factors. Sugar maples require relatively warm winters and fairly deep soil to survive, both of which are rare in northern Minnesota. Maples can't survive below -40 °. The thermal mass of Lake Superior keeps the north shore cool in the summer, but also keeps the area warm in winter. Maples thrive on the ridgelines, but not in the adjacent valleys, into which cold air sinks. The maple forests get their deep soil as a gift from two different glaciers which advanced parallel to each other, on both sides of the ridgeline, leaving enough glacial till on the ridges for this beautiful, out-of-place forest to thrive.

Highway 1 to Lake County Road 6

START (END)
State Hwy. 1, 0.8 miles north of Illgen City

END (START)
Lake Co. Rd. 6 (Little Marais Rd.), north of Little Marais

LENGTH OF TRAIL SECTION
6.8 miles

SAFETY CONCERNS
• On several sections the SHT runs along the edges of cliffs

• Steep sections of trail slippery when wet

ACCESS AND PARKING
Nearest Hwy. 61 milepost: 59.3

Secondary road name and number: Hwy. 1

Etc: Go north on Hwy. 1 0.8 miles. Parking lot on left, marked with sign. Space for 6 cars. Overnight okay.

FACILITIES
At starting trailhead (farthest southwest): none

Designated campsites on this section of SHT: two

SYNOPSIS
This section, one of the most challenging, varies greatly from easy, long stretches along the contours to steep, scrambling ascents and descents. There are many open ledges affording beautiful views of both Lake Superior and its shoreline, and inland lakes, mountains and valleys. The trail is mostly dry and winds through pockets of maples.

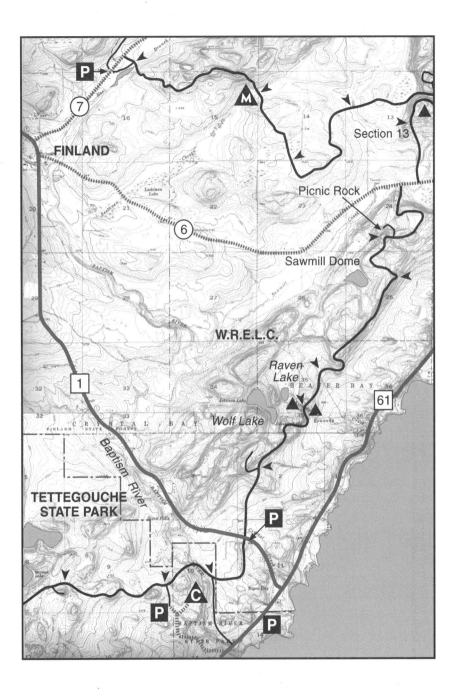

P

7

FINLAND

M

Section 13

Picnic Rock

6

Sawmill Dome

W.R.E.L.C.

Raven
Lake

1

Wolf Lake

61

TETTEGOUCHE
STATE PARK

Baptism River

P

P

C

P

P

MILE-BY-MILE DESCRIPTION

0.0 (6.8)
STATE HWY. 1
SHT crosses Crystal Creek and enters a May 1990 burned area of birch and aspen, with a sign. SHT crosses gravel logging road and traverses wet area. Note Sawtooth summits ahead. SHT soon climbs toward these summits.

0.9 (5.9)
SPUR TRAIL TO OVERLOOKS
The overlooks begin 100 yards up the spur trail, 600 feet above Hwy. 1, the Lake, Palisade Head, Mt. Trudee, and the Silver Bay Harbor. Spur continues for 1/4 mile to more high bluffs. The adjacent landowner calls this area "Fantasia," with vertical cliffs and a beaver pond below. SHT continues downhill from the overlook trail, levels out in a valley where it briefly shares an old road, then rises sharply to open ledges with view of Lake. SHT turns away from Lake, drops a bit, and then climbs switchbacks to an overlook above Wolf Lake, a beautiful lake deep in a depression, originally known as Johnson Lake. From the overlook, SHT curves around the peak, descends, then climbs again to a ridgeline overlooking the Lake.

2.3 (4.5)
KENNEDY CREEK CAMPSITES
SHT heads back into the woods to West Kennedy Creek Campsite. SHT continues across bridge, past spur trail that leads inland to Wolf Ridge Environmental Learning Center. East Kennedy Creek Campsite on a short spur opposite WRELC spur. SHT climbs to a small dome. Just before the steep section, a spur trail leads downward toward Lake. From the dome, SHT descends again.

▲ **WEST KENNEDY CREEK CAMPSITE**

TYPE: Regular
TENT PADS: 5
WATER: From Kennedy Creek
SETTING: 2.3 miles east of Hwy. 1, within Wolf Ridge ELC boundaries
PREVIOUS CAMPSITE: 7.8 miles
NEXT CAMPSITE: 0.1 mile

▲ EAST KENNEDY CREEK CAMPSITE

TYPE: Regular
TENT PADS: 6
WATER: From Kennedy Creek
SETTING: 2.4 miles east of Hwy. 1
PREVIOUS CAMPSITE: 0.1 mile
NEXT CAMPSITE: 5.8 miles

2.9 (3.9)
POWERLINE
100 yards before powerline, SHT crosses old Johnson Lake Rd., also XC trail leading inland to Wolf Ridge. SHT continues and climbs to an expansive view of Lake, Fantasia, Mystical Mtn. and Marshall Mtn. SHT follows cliff line before it parallels the lake on a high ridge, with fleeting glimpses of Lake. Pass through two big rocks.

4.7 (2.1)
OVERLOOK
From overlook, SHT turns sharply inland towards Sawmill Dome, and remains level and easy through maple woods until a last rise to the top of Sawmill Dome. This large cliff is studded with large pines and overlooks a maple forest, farmsteads, and buildings of Wolf Ridge ELC. Sawmill Dome and Sawmill Creek in the valley below are named after the turn-of-the-century Warren Sawmill in Little Marais.

6.0 (0.8)
SAWMILL DOME
SHT skirts Sawmill Dome with steep cliffs, then descends sharply, past a spur trail (marked unofficially "to picnic place – rock overhang") which goes 150 yards to a semi-cave at base of cliffs. SHT continues to an overlook of Sawmill Creek valley, old Air Force radar base, and Co. Rd. 6, then descends. Climb briefly up log and rock steps to a hilltop with views of Lake and ridgeline. Descend past stone steps and wildlife opening.

6.8 (0.0)
LAKE CO. RD. 6 (LITTLE MARAIS RD.)
Parking lot is 0.4 mile east on Co. Rd. 6, in gravel pit. SHT continues on other side of road between this trailhead and parking lot.

Lake County Road 6 to Finland Recreation Center

START (END)
Lake Co. Rd. 6 (Little Marais Rd.), north of Little Marais

END (START)
Finland Recreation Center, 1.3 miles east of Finland on Lake Co. Rd. 7 (Cramer Rd.)

LENGTH OF TRAIL SECTION
7.6 miles

SAFETY CONCERNS
• Cliffs at Section 13

• Boardwalk at beaver dam

• Water at Leskinen Creek campsite is of poor quality

ACCESS AND PARKING
Nearest Hwy. 61 milepost: 65.3

Secondary road name: Lake Co. Rd. 6 (Little Marais Road)

Etc. Go 2.1 miles on Lake Co. Rd. 6 to parking lot on right in gravel pit. Trailhead is 0.2 miles west on Co. Rd. 6. Many parking spaces available in near end of gravel pit. Overnight okay

FACILITIES
At starting trailhead: none

Designated campsites on this section of SHT: two

SYNOPSIS
This hike leads to some of the more impressive terrain on the SHT, including the high cliffs overlooking the Sawmill Valley, popular with local rock climbers and known to them as "Section 13." There is an impressive boardwalk that has been constructed over a beaver dam and a glacial erratic that is over 20 feet tall. The hike ends with a trek through a valley that includes the east branch of the Baptism River.

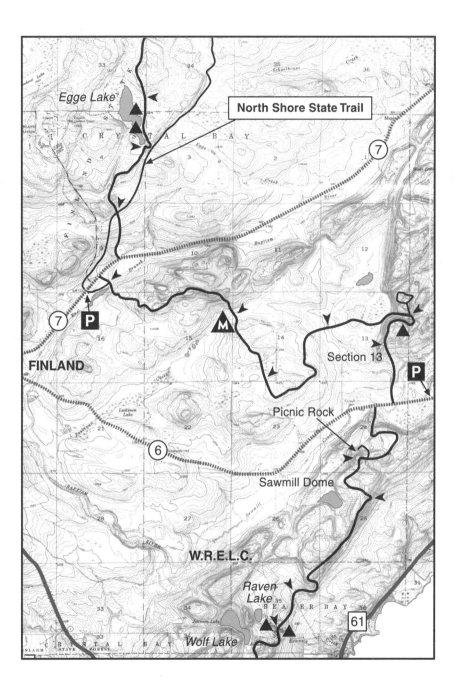

North Shore State Trail

Egge Lake

7

7 P

FINLAND

6

M

Section 13

P

Picnic Rock

Sawmill Dome

W.R.E.L.C.

Raven Lake

Wolf Lake

61

MILE-BY-MILE DESCRIPTION

0.0 (7.6)
LAKE CO. RD. 6 (LITTLE MARAIS RD.)

SHT departs from Co. Rd. 6 about 250 yards west of parking lot, and about 500 yards east of where SHT comes in from Hwy. 1. SHT enters dark spruce and birch forest, then across corduroy through alder. SHT crosses Sawmill Creek and another small creek on newly constructed bridges. SHT climbs gradually along a fir- and spruce-lined ridge, past a beaver pond. At first there are scattered maples, but as the SHT climbs, the maples take over. This may be due to the cold valley air, which is too cold for maple, giving way to the warmer air on the ridges. SHT climbs steeply.

1.0 (6.6)
FIRST OUTCROP/VIEW

The first view of the valley occurs here. SHT continues up rocky ridgeline. Note the occasional oak trees, a sign of drier microclimates on the ridgelines. In late fall, look for Lake views. A little further up, follow short spur at a trail register to another dramatic view. The widest view comes at the open rocky ridge, a common rock-climbing area known as "Section 13." Views from here of inland ridges, beaver pond, and the old Finland radar base. SHT continues to another rock outcrop (again, with seasonal Lake views), then descends into a cedar-filled gulch.

▲ SECTION 13 CAMPSITE

TYPE: Regular
TENT PADS: 4
WATER: From creek at base of cliffs
SETTING: 1.4 miles from Co. Rd. 6
PREVIOUS CAMPSITE: 5.8 miles
NEXT CAMPSITE: 3.8 miles

1.8 (5.8)
SPUR TO OVERLOOK

This was the SHT until new trail was constructed in 2000. The 0.8 mile spur loop climbs to views of cliffs, then runs above valley to another set of views from a rocky, red pine ridge, before looping back.

SHT descends through cedars along an unnamed creek, then crosses it. Watch footing on descent. Section 13 cliffs tower above the trees. SHT turns south and west through mixed forest over low-lying areas with short boardwalks. SHT proceeds through open logged area to beaver pond.

3.0 (4.6)
BOARDWALK AT BEAVER DAM
SHT crosses 440 feet of boardwalk over dam. There is a bench on the north side, good for a lunch spot. SHT ascends through a logged-out area. Look south here for a great view of the Section 13 hills. SHT continues through open area, then enters mixed forest and passes by a huge glacial erratic. SHT enters recently planted area. Watch out for cross trails. Lots of wildflowers blooming in season. SHT leaves plantation area on northeast side and descends through mixed forest to Park Hill Road.

4.4 (3.2)
PARK HILL ROAD
No parking here. SHT enters bog area with long boardwalks to protect it from foot traffic. Look closely and you might see a Lady Slipper. SHT moves through deciduous forest, across old logging road and descends to Leskinen Campsite and Creek. If camping, be cautious about using the water from the creek due to poor quality.

▲ LESKINEN CREEK CAMPSITE

TYPE: Multi-group
TENT PADS: 6
WATER: from Leskinen Creek
SETTING: 0.8 miles north of Park Hill Rd.
PREVIOUS CAMPSITE: 3.8 miles
NEXT CAMPSITE: 4.7 miles

5.2 (2.4)
LESKINEN CREEK
SHT climbs gradually away from creek through mixed forest, then more steeply. At top of ridge, SHT wanders for 0.2 miles with occasional seasonal views to the right. SHT goes down off ridge, then up to secondary ridge with views to the southwest toward the Sawmill

Dome and Lake. SHT descends to Finland Ski Trail and follows it downhill. Watch for signs. SHT descends to East Branch of Baptism River. Bridge here is shared with the ski trail. SHT goes north along Tower Creek for 0.1 mi. to junction with spur trail. Watch for fish ramp at bridge over Tower Creek. At junction, SHT continues north to Crosby-Manitou State Park.

7.3 (0.3)
JUNCTION WITH SPUR TRAIL
SHT goes north from junction to Co. Rd. 7 and beyond. Spur goes 0.3 miles west through mixed forest to Finland Recreation Center parking lot.

7.6 (0.0)
FINLAND RECREATION CENTER

Finland Recreation Center to Crosby-Manitou State Park

START (END)
Finland Recreation Center, 1.3 miles east of Finland on Lake Co. Rd. 7 (Cramer Rd.)

END (START)
Crosby-Manitou State Park

LENGTH OF TRAIL SECTION
11.8 miles

SAFETY CONCERNS
• Intersections with snowmobile trail

ACCESS AND PARKING
Nearest Hwy. 61 milepost: 65.3

Secondary road name and number: Lake Co. Rd. 6 (Little Marais Rd.) and Lake Co. Rd. 7 (Cramer Rd.)

Etc. From Hwy. 61 go 7.2 miles on Lake Co. Rd. 6 to junction of Hwy. 1. Turn right 0.1 mile and right again on Lake Co. Rd. 7. Go 1.3 miles to parking behind ball field. Overnight okay.

FACILITIES
At starting trailhead: outhouses at parking lot

Designated campsites on this section of the SHT: seven

SYNOPSIS
This section, while longer, is relatively level hiking. It offers a wide variety of terrain and forest types. SHT passes through mixed hardwood forests, groves of large cedar, excellent moose habitat and past two spectacular inland lakes. Unique features of this section are the old trapper's cabin and the boardwalk to the island on Sonju Lake.

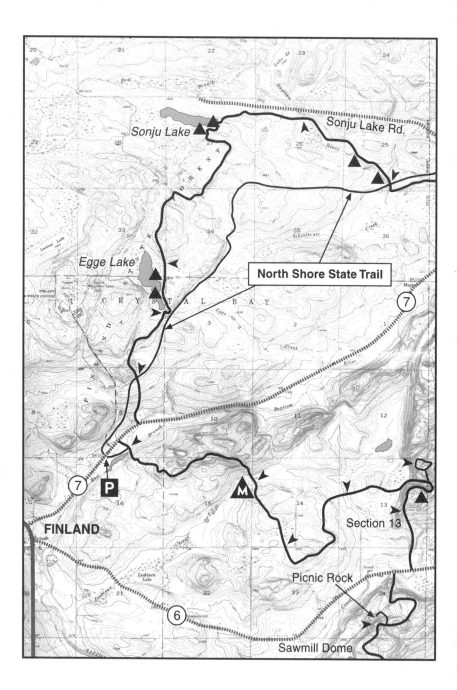

Sonju Lake

Sonju Lake Rd.

North Shore State Trail

Egge Lake

CRYSTAL BAY

7

7

P

FINLAND

M

6

Section 13

Picnic Rock

Sawmill Dome

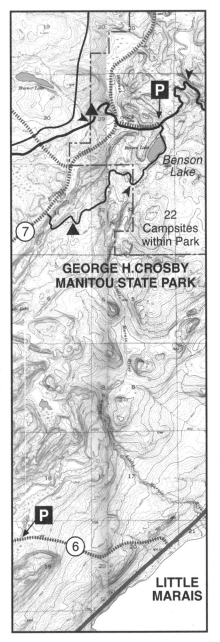

MILE-BY-MILE DESCRIPTION

0.0 (11.8)
PARKING LOT
From the parking lot, a 0.3 mile spur leads to the main SHT. SHT crosses Co. Rd. 7 and follows the road for 0.2 mile then enters a mixed hardwood forest and climbs. SHT crosses an old logging road before coming to North Shore State Trail.

1.1 (10.7)
NORTH SHORE STATE TRAIL
SHT crosses the North Shore State Trail, route of the John Beargrease Sled Dog Marathon each winter, and continues through mixed forest of birch, balsam fir and cedar. SHT follows over 200 feet of boardwalk, then continues ascent. SHT crosses unnamed creek, ascends then curves to left; look for abandoned bear den on left. The forest becomes predominantly maple.

2.3 (9.5)
EGGE LAKE
SHT reaches Egge Lake, then follows Egge Creek steeply downhill to a spur trail that leads to North Shore State Trail. SHT crosses the creek over a scenic gorge, then doubles back toward Egge Lake. SHT continues along ridge above Egge Lake. Past the South and

North Egge Lake campsites, SHT passes under tree that forms a natural arch and continues through a maple forest.

▲ SOUTH EGGE LAKE CAMPSITE

TYPE: Regular
TENT PADS: 4
WATER: From Egge Lake
SETTING: On lake shore with view of opposite shore
PREVIOUS CAMPSITE: 4.7 miles
NEXT CAMPSITE: 0.2 mile

▲ NORTH EGGE LAKE CAMPSITE

TYPE: Regular
TENT PADS: 4
WATER: From Egge Lake
SETTING: On lake shore
PREVIOUS CAMPSITE: 0.2 mile
NEXT CAMPSITE: 3.1 miles

3.0 (8.8)
OLD TRAPPER'S CABIN

SHT passes right by an old trapper's cabin. This is a unique historical feature—please use care when observing so as not to disturb or harm the site. Watch out for broken glass on the ground. After leaving the cabin SHT enters a cedar grove. Observe the numbers on the trees; this was most likely a study site in the past. SHT passes a natural rock ledge bench then turns and climbs away from Egge Lake, descends into a ravine, then climbs again.

4.4 (7.4)
BEAVER POND

SHT crosses boardwalk over beaver pond and follows around the pond. The beaver lodge is visible at a turn in the trail. SHT ascends from beaver pond through alternating cedar and maple forests.

5.9 (5.9)
SOUTH SONJU LAKE CAMPSITE

SHT turns onto a ridge that overlooks Sonju Lake then descends to the lake shore. An 80-foot boardwalk leads to a small island with a view to the end of the lake.

▲ SOUTH SONJU LAKE CAMPSITE

TYPE: Regular
TENT PADS: 4
WATER: From Sonju Lake
SETTING: 200 feet from lake shore
PREVIOUS CAMPSITE: 3.1 miles
NEXT CAMPSITE: 0.3 mile

▲ NORTH SONJU LAKE CAMPSITE

TYPE: Regular
TENT PADS: 4
WATER: From Sonju Lake—dock allows easy access to water
SETTING: On lake shore
PREVIOUS CAMPSITE: 0.3 mile
NEXT CAMPSITE: 1.9 miles

6.2 (5.6)
SONJU CREEK

After crossing Sonju Creek, SHT leaves cedar grove and enters logged area with immature spruce, then descends to an 80-foot boardwalk, re-enters a cedar forest, then comes to an open, rocky area with a valley below. The valley is prime moose habitat. Next, SHT crosses a logging road into a plantation area of white spruce.

7.5 (4.3)
EAST BRANCH BAPTISM RIVER CROSSING

SHT crosses the river and continues downstream. To the left is a spur trail to a parking area on Sonju Lake Rd. SHT continues right along the bank of the river.

▲ EAST BRANCH BAPTISM RIVER CAMPSITE

TYPE: Regular
TENT PADS: 4
WATER: From river
SETTING: On river bank
PREVIOUS CAMPSITE: 1.9 miles
NEXT CAMPSITE: 0.6 mile

▲ **BLESNER CREEK CAMPSITE**

TYPE: Regular
TENT PADS: 4
WATER: From river or creek
SETTING: In cedar grove at intersection of creek and river
PREVIOUS CAMPSITE: 0.6 mile
NEXT CAMPSITE: 2.1 miles

8.7 (3.1)
BLESNER CREEK

Blesner Creek flows from Blesner Lake, named for an early 20th century homesteader. Blesner Creek enters the East Branch Baptism River in a cedar grove. SHT again crosses the North Shore State Trail next to a bridge across the river and soon heads away from the river through a mixed forest before crossing Sonju Lake Rd.

10.6 (1.2)
BLESNER LAKE ROAD

SHT crosses Blesner Lake Road and passes Aspen Knob campsite. SHT climbs to a knoll overlooking the Baptism River valley before descending to Lake Co. Rd. 7. SHT crosses the road and follows the entrance road to Crosby-Manitou State Park.

▲ **ASPEN KNOB CAMPSITE**

TYPE: Regular
TENT PADS: 3
WATER: From unnamed creek 300 feet away on SHT
SETTING: On a knob adjacent to the SHT
PREVIOUS CAMPSITE: 2.1 miles
NEXT CAMPSITE: 5.1 miles on main SHT (or 3.1 on Benson Lake spur trail)

11.8 (0.0)
CROSBY-MANITOU STATE PARK TRAILHEAD

MILE-BY-MILE DESCRIPTION:
SPUR TRAIL FROM CROSBY-MANITOU STATE PARK TO BENSON LAKE AND DISAPPEARING POND CAMPSITE

0.0 (2.6)
CROSBY-MANITOU PARKING LOT

Spur leaves from parking lot on State Park's Benson Lake Trail and follows west side of Benson Lake.

0.8 (1.8)
SPUR LEAVES STATE PARK TRAIL

Spur turns northwest along a typical Lake Superior Highland ridge, including the maple forests. Watch for the "disappearing" pond to the east.

2.0 (0.6)
CAMPSITE

▲ **DISAPPEARING POND CAMPSITE**

TYPE: Regular
TENT PADS: 3
WATER: From pond
SETTING: 2.0 miles from Crosby-Manitou State Park Parking Lot

2.6 (0.0)
END OF SPUR TRAIL

Spur trail ends here. Private property ahead—please stay off. Return to Crosby-Manitou State Park.

PROTECTING EGGE LAKE

The land around Crosby-Manitou State Park and Egge Lake has been bouncing quickly around from one landowner to another recently. Only in this land swap game, everybody wins.

The rolling landscape of Egge Lake is part of a 700-acre parcel that was privately owned until 1999. The Nature Conservancy of Minnesota had an option to buy it, but offered this option to the Parks and Trails Council of Minnesota. The Council is a non-profit group that, according to its mission statement, "acts to help establish, develop and enhance Minnesota's parks and trails, and to encourage their protection and enjoyment." The Council bought the land, to swap for land owned by Lake County but held within the boundary of Crosby Manitou State Park. The Egge Lake parcel is to become county forest, and the park's holdings will get bigger.

The end result is that this beautiful tract of northern hardwood forest will be preserved within a larger county forest management scheme. Left to private ownership, this inland lake could have been developed with roads and cabins. Collaboration between businesses, nonprofit groups and government saved the day.

Crosby-Manitou State Park to Caribou River Wayside

START (END)
Crosby-Manitou State Park, off Lake Co. Rd. 7 (Cramer Rd.)

END (START)
Caribou River State Wayside, on Hwy. 61

LENGTH OF TRAIL SECTION
8.0 miles

SAFETY CONCERNS
• Deep gorges and cliffs at Caribou and Manitou rivers

ACCESS AND PARKING
Nearest Hwy. 61 milepost: either 59.3 for Hwy. 1 or 65.3 for Lake Co. Rd. 6

Secondary road name and number: follow either road to Finland and continue north on Hwy. 1 just past the junction with Co. Rd. 6. Turn right onto Co. Rd. 7, 8 miles to the entrance of Crosby-Manitou State Park. Approximately 30 parking spaces at state park (state park permit required). Overnight okay.

FACILITIES
At starting trailhead (farthest southwest): outhouses

Designated campsites on this section of the SHT: 22 in Crosby-Manitou State Park (requires sign-in and fee); two on SHT

SYNOPSIS
This section of the SHT is quite dramatic in terms of topography, offering broad views of both inland ridges, ponds, and rivers, and of Lake Superior. The SHT here is more rugged than most sections and visits a variety of forest habitats. The western half of the section skirts the valley of the wild Manitou River, while the eastern half explores the cedar groves of the Little Manitou drainage and the dramatic Caribou River gorge.

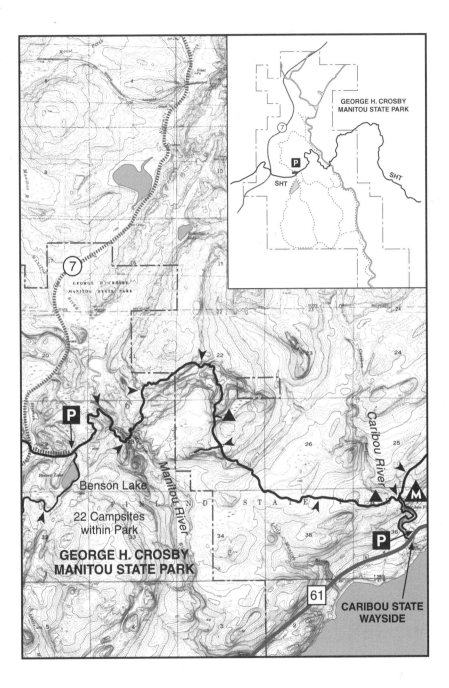

MILE-BY-MILE DESCRIPTION

0.0 (8.0)
PARKING LOT

SHT leaves from parking lot at mapboard on the "Middle Trail," into semi-mature birch forest, past a large glacial erratic and across plank bridges. Spur on downhill side leads 70 yards to view of Lake and Manitou River valley. SHT descends steeply through cedars, past junction with Crosby Hill Trail.

0.9 (7.1)
JUNCTION OF SHT/MIDDLE TRAIL WITH RIVER TRAIL

Upriver from this junction about 1/4 mile are the Manitou Cascades, a worthy side trip. At junction, SHT goes downriver (right), past state park campsites 3 and 4, and up and over two bluffs with partial overlooks on river valley. Signpost marks where SHT goes downhill to the bridge, descending through a dark spruce forest and an overlook trail 100 yards before the river and bridge. The overlook allows glimpses through the forest of the tumbling river as it descends toward the bridge.

1.6 (6.4)
BRIDGE OVER MANITOU RIVER

Manitou River is one of the most rugged river valleys along the shore. SHT runs steeply past white pine on east side of valley, then into scrubby mixed woods of fir, birch, and aspen. The climb is just 600 yards long but 300 feet up. SHT passes a series of four overlooks with views of the Lake and the Manitou River valley.

2.3 (5.7)
VIEW OF POND

After climbing short rocky slope, view pond and birch/balsam hill behind it. Look for a variety of lichens growing on the rock. Next overlook includes Lake and old Air Force radar base near Finland (white buildings). SHT continues along hilltop, alternating between maple woods and stunning views of the Lake. Note juneberry trees and sumac at the rocky openings. Beaver ponds are visible below. SHT eventually descends again into a deep fault line valley.

3.4 (4.6)
BEAVER STREAM CROSSING ON SMALL BEAVER DAM

SHT then climbs away from river through balsam, birch, and cedar. Forest changes over to maple, then birch and spruce. A series of overlooks on the Little Manitou, the Finland radar base, and spectacular maple hillsides. This area is known as "Horseshoe Ridge." Rock underfoot changes to crumbly rotting lava flow. SHT passes cedar and white pine. Spur near small footbridge goes to campsite, 150 yards.

▲ HORSESHOE RIDGE CAMPSITE

TYPE: Regular
TENT PADS: 2
WATER: From small creek just
   E. of campsite
SETTING: 4.0 miles from Crosby-
   Manitou parking lot, on ridge
   overlooking Manitou River Valley
PREVIOUS CAMPSITE: 5.1 miles
   (or use Crosby-Manitou State Park
   campsites)
NEXT CAMPSITE: 3.1 miles

4.7 (3.3)
SPUR TO OVERLOOK

Spur leads 500 yards to wide view of Manitou, Little Manitou drainages, Lake, and ridges. SHT leads to another expansive view. Look for oaks on this long, rocky ridge. After descending and another view, SHT continues through cedar swamp with plank

GEORGE H. CROSBY-MANITOU STATE PARK

George H. Crosby-Manitou State Park is known for its rugged beauty and fine fishing. The wild and scenic Manitou River runs through the park on its descent to Lake Superior. George Crosby, an early mining magnate, donated the property for use as a state park with the provision that development be limited. With his wishes in mind, the first backpack-only park was designed. Today visitors camp at one of many remote backpack sites located mainly along the river. Hikers self-register for sites at the camping registration board near the camp office. There are 23 miles of trails, and fishing—especially for trout along the river or on Benson Lake—is among the most popular park uses. Because of the relatively undisturbed nature of the park it is common to encounter a variety of wildlife, such as deer and moose, or less frequently, timber wolf, vole, mink, and pileated woodpecker.

walkways. Look for logged-over open area—a good spot for birdwatching.

6.2 (1.8)
LOGGING ROAD

Road built by Bob Silver for selectively cutting cedar in this area. SHT moves into birch/balsam woods, then a small rock outcrop and through spruces and bracken ferns. Between the logging road and the Caribou River, the SHT crosses the historic Pork Bay Trail, a Native American and voyageur trail that led from Pork Bay nine miles inland to Nine-mile Lake. Listen for the Caribou River as the SHT descends. At the river the SHT turns left, upriver. Spur trail descends west side of river to Hwy. 61.

▲ WEST CARIBOU RIVER CAMPSITE

TYPE: Regular
TENT PADS: 4
WATER: From Caribou River
SETTING: 1.0 mile from
   Caribou Wayside parking
PREVIOUS CAMPSITE:
   3.1 miles
NEXT CAMPSITE: 0.3 mile

BRIDGES ON THE SUPERIOR HIKING TRAIL

Some of the trail's most remarkable construction involves bridgework. Each stream that crosses the SHT is bridged, so hikers don't have to get wet or ford rivers. Approximately 40 bridges of various lengths, materials, and construction link embankments and landscapes. Although bridges are vital to trail layout, the best crossing is not always the most convenient place to build. A volunteer crew can make small wooden walkways from nearby resources, but some bridges are elaborately designed and need the transport of considerable lumber and other materials. The Baptism River suspension bridge, for example, required helicopter transport of supplies because of its complexity and location. Some bridges, like the one at Lake Agnes, were made during the winter, when larger timbers could be dragged across the ice. The Manitou River Bridge has a unique laminated stringer technique—at 40 feet, this is the longest possible bridge built with this technique.

7.3 (0.7)
BRIDGE OVER CARIBOU RIVER
Trail junction on east side of bridge. Spur runs downstream to
Caribou Falls and Hwy. 61 parking lot. SHT continues upstream to
Cook Co. Rd. 1. Along spur trail, keep an eye on river as it cascades
through narrow stone walls. Sign marks where spur trail forks, with
the river-side fork going on narrow path down to gorgeous falls then
downriver, the other fork straight to Hwy. 61 along top of bluff. Listen
for the falls if you get confused.

8.1 (0.0)
CARIBOU WAYSIDE (HWY. 61)
Mileage sign marks trailhead.

Caribou River Wayside to Cook County Road 1

START (END)
Caribou River State Wayside on Hwy. 61

END (START)
Cook Co. Rd. 1 (Cramer Rd.)

LENGTH OF TRAIL SECTION
9.0 miles

SAFETY CONCERNS
• Floating bog at Alfred's Pond

• Active railroad tracks

ACCESS AND PARKING
Nearest Hwy. 61 milepost: 70.5

Secondary road name and number: none

Etc: Parking lot is on north side of highway. Space for 10 cars. No overnight parking allowed at state wayside.

FACILITIES
At starting trailhead (farthest southwest): none

Designated campsites on this section of the SHT: four

SYNOPSIS
After ascending the beautiful and dramatic Caribou River gorge, this section of the SHT follows a series of ridges and overlooks through mixed deciduous woods. The bog vegetation of the Alfred's Pond area is a quiet highlight. Lots of evidence of logging, including roads and clearcuts, helps the hiker understand the role of logging in forest ecology. Although this section is lengthy, it is one of the easier sections to hike—perfect for a long nature walk, with an abundance of wildflowers.

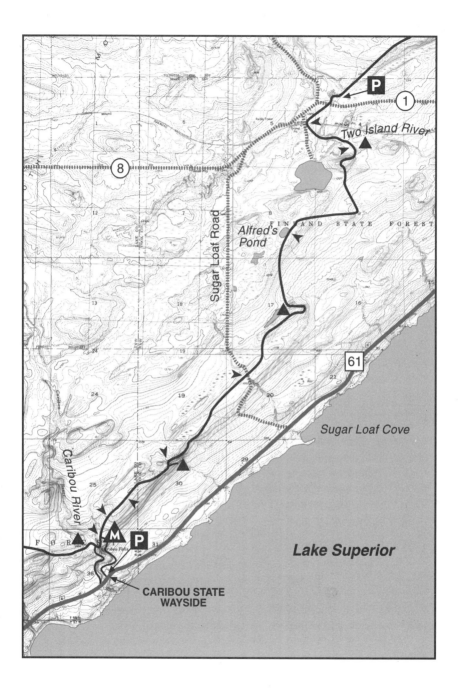

Lake Superior

Sugar Loaf Cove

Alfred's Pond

Two Island River

Sugar Loaf Road

Caribou River

CARIBOU STATE WAYSIDE

MILE-BY-MILE DESCRIPTION

0.0 (9.0)
PARKING LOT OFF HWY. 61
There are two spur trails which connect with the SHT above Caribou Falls. West Spur Trail: Leaves from south side of Caribou River Wayside across river. Spur climbs to ridge over eroded area, goes down to riverside, then gradually climbs to view of falls at ridge level. Continue climbing along side of river gorge to junction with main SHT. East Spur Trail: Leaves from north end of parking lot. Within 1/4 mile there is a trail junction. Right leads around falls directly to SHT. Left leads to base of Caribou Falls, then rejoins main spur trail at 0.5 miles. After two forks of spur rejoin, the east spur continues along gorge of Caribou River through pine and spruce.

0.7 (8.3)
JUNCTION WITH MAIN SHT
Note bridge across Caribou River. Spur trail to campsite just away from river. Past campsite, SHT follows small stream, then through a clear-cut area.

🏕 EAST CARIBOU RIVER CAMPSITE

TYPE: Multi-group
TENT PADS: 8
WATER: From Caribou River
SETTING: 0.7 mile from Caribou Wayside parking lot, near the Caribou River bridge crossing
PREVIOUS CAMPSITE: 0.3 mile
NEXT CAMPSITE: 1.2 miles

1.2 (7.8)
LOGGING ROAD
Look carefully for SHT sign across road. Good view of Lake. SHT follows ridge, along logging road and then re-enters mixed hardwoods and birch forest after powerline, with seasonal view of Lake.

2.0 (7.0)
SPUR TO CAMPSITE
Right after campsite spur, SHT crosses Crystal Creek, then enters marvelous birch forest. If you want, follow Crystal Creek down a ways to a

collapsed mine shaft. At this mine, note the wide band of calcite crystals in the bottom of the creek's gorge. These crystals led a prospector to believe there would be ore there also. SHT passes through large birch forest, crosses powerline and private road and passes through old Consolidated Paper plantations on private land.

▲ CRYSTAL CREEK CAMPSITE

TYPE: Regular
TENT PADS: 4
WATER: From Crystal Creek
SETTING: 1.5 miles west of
 Sugarloaf Rd., 350 feet
 off SHT
PREVIOUS CAMPSITE: 1.2 miles
NEXT CAMPSITE: 2.4 miles

3.5 (5.5)
SUGARLOAF RD.

After crossing road past parking lot and sign, SHT winds up and down ridge, with glimpses of the Lake, then an area with signs of an old fire. This is the most difficult hiking of the section. SHT enters mixed maple and aspen woods, then a swampy wet section.

4.5 (4.5)
POND CAMPSITE

SHT continues, across logging road and Alfred's Pond Rd.

BOGS ON THE TRAIL

Bogs are a type of wetland common in northern Minnesota, though less common along the Superior Hiking Trail. Bogs are characterized by a lush growth of sphagnum moss and high acidity. Since the bog is a nutrient-poor environment, some bog plants have evolved insect eating as a way of getting needed nutrients like nitrogen. The pitcher plant and sundew are two insectivorous plants common in the bogs in northern Minnesota.

The sundew is a tiny plant usually found on the edge of the mat close to water. It has sticky tipped hairs on its leaves that trap insects. The pitcher plant is much bigger, perhaps a foot across, and traps insects in its hollow, fluid-filled leaves. Bogs are fascinating places to explore, but please use the boardwalk if provided.

▲ POND CAMPSITE

TYPE: Regular
TENT PADS: 4
WATER: pond
SETTING: 1.0 mile east of Sugarloaf Rd.
PREVIOUS CAMPSITE: 2.4 miles
NEXT CAMPSITE: 3.5 miles

5.8 (3.2)
ALFRED'S POND

Look for bog plants like the carnivorous pitcher plant and sundew, as well as sphagnum moss, orchids, and blue-flag iris. Floating walkway built in 1992 allows one to see everything without getting wet or damaging the bog. After pond, there's some boggy walking. SHT climbs uphill, with possible view of Dyer's Lake through trees and, at 6.7 miles, of Lake Superior, then a steep downhill into birch valley.

7.9 (1.1)
DYER'S CREEK CAMPSITE

After crossing Dyer's Creek on a 25-foot footbridge, look for trail on right side of SHT to campsite. SHT continues upstream on south bank of Two Island River, then ascends steeply through mixed conifers.

▲ DYER'S CREEK CAMPSITE

TYPE: Regular
TENT PADS: 4
WATER: From Dyer's Creek
SETTING: 1.1 miles west of Co. Rd. 1
PREVIOUS CAMPSITE: 3.5 miles
NEXT CAMPSITE: 2.9 miles

8.6 (0.4)
1ST ROAD CROSSING

SHT meets or crosses, in order: Dyer's Lake Rd, active railroad tracks that lead to Taconite Harbor, woods, Cook Co. Rd. 1, gravel pit road, Two Island River, then parking area.

9.0 (0.0)
PARKING AREA OFF COOK CO. RD. 1 (CRAMER RD.)

WILDFLOWER CALENDAR FOR THE SUPERIOR HIKING TRAIL

MAY

Bloodroot	*Sanguinaria canadensis*
Violets	*Viola*
Wild Lily-of-the-Valley	*Maianthemum canadense*
Common Strawberry	*Fuagaria virginiana*
Marsh-marigold	*Caltha palustris*
Spring Beauty	*Claytonia virginica*
Wood Anemone	*Anemone quinquefolia*
Goldthread	*Coptis groenlandica*

JUNE

Nodding Trillium	*Trillium cernuum*
Starflower	*Trientalis borealis*
Bunchberry	*Cornus canadensis*
Columbine	*Aquilegia canadensis*
Moccasin Flower	*Cypripedium acaule*
Larger Blue-flag	*Iris versicolor*
Blue-bead Lily	*Clintonia borealis*

JULY

Meadowsweet	*Spiraea latifolia*
Spreading Dogbane	*Apocynum androsaemifolium*
Northern Bedstraw	*Galium boreale*
Indian-pipe	*Monotropa uniflora*
Heal-all	*Prunella vulgaris*
Cow-parsnip	*Heracleum maximum*

AUGUST

Goldenrods	*Solidago*
Large-leaf Aster	*Aster macrophyllus*
Fireweed	*Epilobium angustifolium*
Jewelweed	*Impatiens capensis*
Evening Primrose	*Oenothera*
Spotted Joe-Pye-Weed	*Eupatorium maculatum*

Cook County Road 1 to Temperance River State Park

START (END)
SHT parking lot on Cook Co. Rd. 1

END (START)
Either Temperance River State Park parking lot on Hwy. 61 or SHT parking lot on Forest Rd. 343

LENGTH OF TRAIL SECTION
8.0 miles

ACCESS AND PARKING
TRAILHEAD #1
Nearest Hwy. 61 milepost: 78.9

Secondary road name and number: Cook Co. Rd. 1 (Cramer Rd.)

Etc: Go northwest on Cook Co. Rd. 1 for 3.6 miles (first 1.7 miles paved, rest is gravel). Lot is on right 200' off Co. Rd. 1 and 0.1 miles before SHT crossing. Space for 7–8 cars. Overnight okay.

ACCESS AND PARKING
TRAILHEAD #2
Nearest Hwy. 61 milepost: 79.1

Secondary road name and number: Skou Rd. directly across from a former gas station.

Etc.: Go 0.2 miles from Hwy. 61. Park by trailhead. Space for 3 cars. Overnight okay.

FACILITIES
At starting trailhead (farthest southwest): none

Bathrooms, water, and telephone at the Cross River Cafe

Designated campsites on this section of the SHT: three

SYNOPSIS
This section of the SHT offers a comprehensive look at the steep character of the region's watershed. The climb to Tower Overlook, the descent to Fredenberg Creek, and the hike along the marsh set the stage for the highlight of the section, the historic Cross River. Also, there is ample evidence of both recent and historical logging.

MILE-BY-MILE DESCRIPTION

0.0 (8.0)
PARKING LOT

SHT has come 0.2 miles through the woods from crossing Co. Rd. 1. SHT continues from the left side of the lot. SHT passes through old clearcut area, then into the Northern Hardwood Research and Natural Area. Note conifers in low area on both sides. SHT climbs to Tower Overlook, with a beautiful view of Lake, then descends.

1.8 (6.2)
FREDENBERG CREEK

100 feet after footbridge, spur trail to campsite on south side of SHT, near sharp turn. SHT follows creek, then follows edge of marsh, known locally as Boney's Meadow. This is a wonderful place to view waterfowl. Look for moose tracks near marsh.

▲ **FREDENBERG CREEK CAMPSITE**

TYPE: Regular
TENT PADS: 4
WATER: From Fredenberg Creek
SETTING: 1.8 miles east of Co. Rd. 1
PREVIOUS CAMPSITE: 2.9 miles
NEXT CAMPSITE: 3.5 miles

LOGGING ON THE NORTH SHORE

Logging started on the North Shore in the 1880s, after pine forests to the east had been logged. Large stands of tall white and red pine were harvested, then transported by horse-pulled sleighs in winter and open water-ways in spring and summer down to the Lake for transport to sawmills in Duluth and Ashland. The 1920s saw trucks and tractors bringing down black and white spruce for paper and lumber, and then secondary trees such as aspen, birch, and cedar for paper and other forest products. This fifty-year period of timber removal, transportation develop-ment, and human settlement drastically changed the wood-lands along the North Shore. Following the depletion of the tall pines, the logging industry necessarily began sustained-yield logging to ensure renewable resources. The logged areas you see from the trail are part of a developing conservation move-ment emphasizing stewardship and recognizing the forest's timber, wildlife, and recreational qualities.

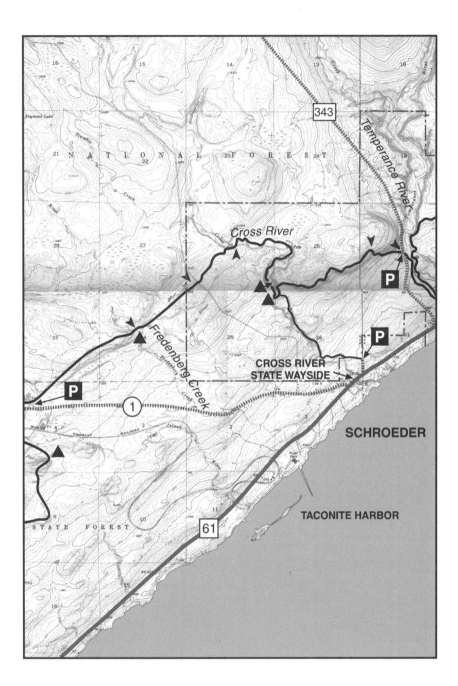

343

Temperance River

Cross River

NATIONAL FOREST

Dogwood Lake

P

P

CROSS RIVER
STATE WAYSIDE

Fredenberg Creek

P

1

SCHROEDER

STATE FOREST

TACONITE HARBOR

61

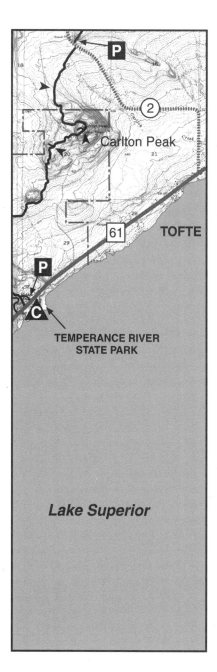

TOFTE

TEMPERANCE RIVER
STATE PARK

Lake Superior

HISTORY OF THE CROSS RIVER

Hugging the banks of this spirited little river for over a mile, the SHT gives ample opportunity to observe the various antics of the rushing water—site of any number of interesting historical events. The Voyageurs portaged this stretch of rapids to reach the calm headwaters, a chain of inland lakes, and eventually Lake Vermilion, near Tower. By the turn of the century, loggers had entered the watershed and used the river for the roaring spring log drive down to the boom at the mouth. This included putting a series of dams on the river. So "roaring" was the river that there are accounts of a bordello in what is now Schroeder. The logging business ceased operations in 1905 due in part to a smallpox epidemic.

2.9 (5.1)
GASCO RD.
This is a historic logging road, also a spur to the North Shore State Trail, a multipurpose trail linking Duluth and Grand Marais. SHT enters new-growth evergreens, probably an 80-acre clearcut replanted with white spruce in the 1970s, then a hardwood forest, then descends to a lowland. SHT then reaches the bluff of the Cross River.

3.8 (4.2)
FALLS ON CROSS RIVER
Great view of falls, excellent lunch or rest stop. The river is definitely the highlight of this section. SHT follows edge of river up and down small bluffs. Look for beaver activity on sidestreams.

5.3 (2.7)
CROSS RIVER CAMPSITES AND BRIDGE
Note campsites on both sides of SHT. Trail junction after bridge: SHT goes straight, spur trail 1.5 miles to Schroeder goes downstream. SHT follows bluff, then moves to ridgeline, with views of Lake and Taconite Harbor operations. Note the total absence of red or white pines, evidence of the pine logging operations early this century and their completeness. The large grove of mature red pine on this section was planted for future cutting.

▲ NORTH CROSS RIVER CAMPSITE

TYPE: Regular
TENT PADS: 4
WATER: From Cross River
SETTING: 5.3 miles from Co. Rd. 1, above river
PREVIOUS CAMPSITE: 3.5 miles
NEXT CAMPSITE: 0.0 miles

▲ SOUTH CROSS RIVER CAMPSITE

TYPE: Regular
TENT PADS: 4
WATER: From Cross River
SETTING: 1.5 miles up spur trail from Schroeder, above river
PREVIOUS CAMPSITE: 0.0 miles
NEXT CAMPSITE: 9.1 miles (or use Temperance River State Park)

6.4 (1.6)
TOP OF RIDGE
Long and sometimes steep descent through a typical birch/aspen forest.

7.2 (0.8)
TEMPERANCE RIVER RD. (FOREST RD. 343)
SHT crosses road at parking lot 0.9 miles up Forest Rd. 343 from
Hwy. 61. Either end hike here or continue along Temperance River
into state park. SHT leads downstream as the Temperance changes
from a wide, quiet river to a roaring cascade in narrow gorges. SHT
alternates between woods and bedrock river edge. SHT eventually
joins state park XC trail for about 0.3 mile, then turns sharply left to
follow edge of second gorge for about 200 yards before reaching the
snowmobile bridge across the Temperance cascades. After crossing
bridge, spur trail goes downstream to parking lot; or main SHT goes
upstream to Carlton Peak and beyond.

8.0 (0.0)
TEMPERANCE RIVER STATE PARK PARKING LOT

Temperance River State Park to Britton Peak

START (END)
Temperance River Wayside parking lot on Hwy. 61

END (START)
Britton Peak parking lot on Cook Co. Rd. 2 (Sawbill Trail)

LENGTH OF TRAIL SECTION
4.8 miles

SAFETY CONCERNS
• Cliffs on Carlton Peak

ACCESS AND PARKING
Nearest Hwy. 61 milepost: 80.3
Secondary road name and number: none

Etc: Trailhead is on north side of road, on east side of the river. Look for SHT sign

Space for at least 60 cars. 6 hour limit at parking lot, can park overnight at lot in campground area (permit required).

FACILITIES
Bathrooms, outhouses, telephone, drinking water, campground

Designated campsites on this section of the SHT: none

SYNOPSIS
This is one of the most easily accessible sections of the SHT and one of the most commonly used. The hike to Carlton Peak from either direction is an easy ascent, and the scramble to the top of the peak is a fun adventure with ample rewards of incredible views. Coming from Temperance River State Park, the hiker also gets to see the amazing Temperance River, roaring deep in a dark basaltic canyon.

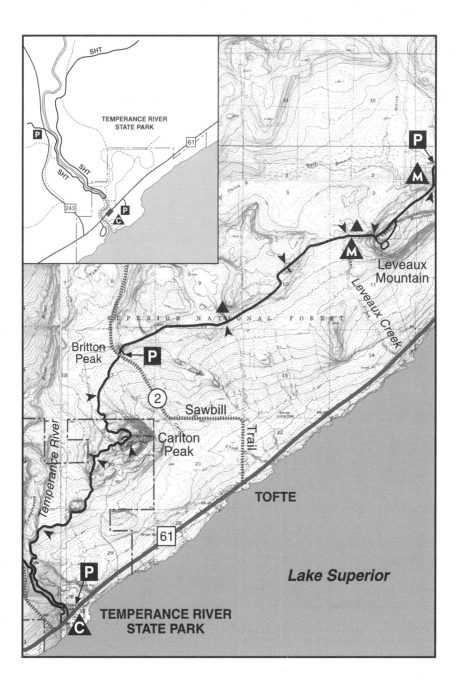

TEMPERANCE RIVER STATE PARK

The Temperance River was presumably so named because, unlike other North Shore streams, this river had no bar at its mouth. The 200 acres at the mouth of the river are now the State Park, which is best known for its deep, narrow river gorge, waterfalls, and the glacial potholes that dot the river valley.

Fishing is popular on the Temperance and nearby Cross Rivers, where several species of trout and salmon have been stocked and have become established. Two campgrounds with a total of 50 sites are popular because of their lakeside location. Eight miles of trails connect with the North Shore State Trail, the SHT and Superior National Forest trails, and provide recreational use year around. Picnic sites are located along Lake Superior adjacent to the lower campground.

MILE-BY-MILE DESCRIPTION

0.0 (4.8)
TRAILHEAD AT STATE PARK PARKING LOT

This is a spur trail which joins the SHT at the snowmobile bridge 0.2 miles up the gorge from the trailhead. Spur and SHT follow "Cauldron Trail" up narrow gorge of river - look for interpretive signs. Trails fork and wander a lot, but SHT continues upstream until the river flattens out, then SHT becomes wide and clear. SHT joins XC trail at a switchback and climbs high on rim over river.

1.2 (3.6)
SHT LEAVES RIVER

SHT enters scrubby woods, then a semi-mature birch forest. The Lynx XC trail follows the SHT. Look for signs of old white pines and fire. Two major fires have swept through here. Look for national forest survey lines, the wide straight cuts through the forest. At one point, SHT turns steeply uphill, leaving XC trail and climbing through birches.

2.6 (2.2)
OVERLOOK SPUR

Look for sign and follow spur 80 yards for a view of Lake, Temperance River valley, and Taconite Harbor. SHT continues, through a solid birch forest, past a spur with an old access road and ski trail to Carlton Peak. SHT begins gradual ascent counterclockwise around Carlton

Peak, through large fallen boulders. This is a popular rock climbing site and the only difficult hiking on this section.

3.1 (1.7)
SPUR TRAIL TO SUMMIT

Well worth the trip to the top. Trail register at the spur trail junction leading to summit on left. Secondary summit known as "Ted Tofte Overlook" on right. Leaving the summit, there are high rock faces on left side of SHT. Watch for view of Britton Peak and Raven's Ridge above Tofte.

4.0 (0.8)
LYNX XC TRAIL

SHT now in maple forest, then an open grassy area, created by the U.S. Forest Service by logging, raking, spraying, and planting spruce. Watch for kestrels, bluebirds, and migrating hawks. Lots of wooden walkways to cross muddy areas. SHT reenters woods, crosses ski trail, then crosses Sawbill Trail and winds into the Britton Peak parking lot.

4.8 (0.0)
BRITTON PEAK PARKING LOT

CARLTON PEAK

The high points on the North Shore landscape exist because they are made of rocks that have been more resistant to weathering and erosion over the billion years since they were formed. Carlton Peak is a prime example, made of several huge blocks of whitish anorthosite rock. These blocks were carried or floated up from the base of the earth's crust, 25 or 30 miles below, suspended in molten diabase magma. With very few natural fractures, these anorthosite blocks or "inclusions" also make up many of the knobs and hills in and around Silver Bay and Tettegouche State Park.

A climb to the top of Carlton Peak reveals some tremendous views, which is why this was the site of a fire tower up until the 1950s (the foundation is all that is left of the tower).

Britton Peak to Oberg Mountain

START (END)
Britton Peak access on Cook Co. Rd. 2 (Sawbill Trail)

END (START)
Oberg Mtn. parking lot on Forest Rd. 336 (Onion River Rd.)

LENGTH OF TRAIL SECTION
5.7 miles

SAFETY CONCERNS
• Continual beaver activity west of Leveaux Mtn.

ACCESS AND PARKING
Nearest Hwy. 61 milepost: 82.8

Secondary road name and number: Cook Co. Rd. 2 (Sawbill Trail)

Etc: Go 2.7 miles north on Sawbill Trail. Parking area on right, 15-20 spaces available. Overnight okay.

FACILITIES
At starting trailhead (farthest southwest): outhouse

Designated campsites on this section of the SHT: four

SYNOPSIS
This section crosses the Sugarbush cross-country ski trail system several times. The section, one of the easier of the SHT, begins as an easy, rolling path through maple and birch forest, with a carpet of leaves underfoot in autumn. The topography becomes more dramatic in the central section and the maple and birch give way to spruce, balsam, and cedar around the beaver pond. From the pond the SHT ascends to the Leveaux Mtn. loop and on to the parking area. Wet and seasonally wet ground is typical along this section.

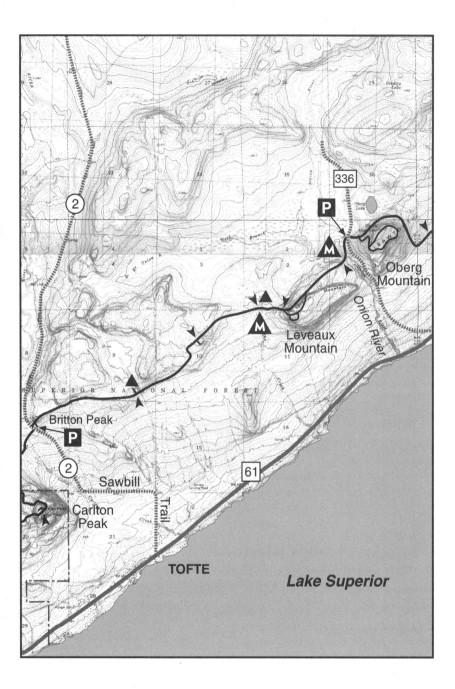

MILE-BY-MILE DESCRIPTION

0.0 (5.7)
PARKING AREA

Right after SHT leaves trailhead, spur leads steeply up to overlook near top of Britton Peak. The view from the top is dominated by Carlton Peak in the distance. There is a memorial for W.L. Britton, a WWII veteran who worked for the Forest Service for two years. His ashes were strewn on Britton Peak in 1947. The SHT crosses ski trails frequently, at 0.2. 1.2, and 1.4 miles. Ski trails have blue blazes, SHT has white blazes. Look for yellow birch curved into "S" shape. SHT also crosses numerous planks and corduroy in wet spots.

1.6 (4.1)
WOODEN BRIDGE

Look for signs of black bears chewing on bridge timbers. SHT campsite just east of bridge. SHT crosses XC trail, then climbs through young sugar maple stand to an overlook with a view of the Lake, Apostle Islands 30 miles away. SHT crosses old roadbed.

▲ SUGAR BUSH CREEK CAMPSITE

TYPE: Regular
TENT PADS: 4
WATER: Unreliable during dry conditions
SETTING: 1.6 miles from Sawbill Trail, just east of bridge.
 View from rock above.
PREVIOUS CAMPSITE: 9.1 miles (or use Temperance River State Park)
NEXT CAMPSITE: 2.5 miles

2.9 (2.8)
SPUR TRAIL TO CEDAR OVERLOOK

Steep 1/8 mile climb to view of Lake and Sawtooth Mtns., including Leveaux, Oberg, and Moose Mtns. SHT continues along ridge, then crosses ski trail. Forest begins to change to spruce and balsam. Lots of diamonds marking XC trails throughout this area.

4.2 (1.5)
BRIDGE ACROSS LEVEAUX BEAVER POND

Look for the beaver lodge to the north, and watch for moose. Beavers are active here, and as a result SHT may be flooded. SHT campsite 0.2 miles past bridge. SHT crosses XC trail, enters cedar grove, then enters maple forest beneath the cliffs of Leveaux Mtn.

⛺ WEST LEVEAUX POND CAMPSITE

TYPE: Multi-group
TENT PADS: 8
WATER: From beaver pond—
  treat before using
SETTING: 1.7 miles to Forest Rd. 336
PREVIOUS CAMPSITE: 2.5 miles
NEXT CAMPSITE: 0.1 mile

▲ EAST LEVEAUX POND CAMPSITE

TYPE: Regular
TENT PADS: 4
WATER: From beaver pond—treat
  before using
SETTING: 1.6 miles to Forest Rd. 336.
  Nice view of beaver pond.
PREVIOUS CAMPSITE: 0.1 mile
NEXT CAMPSITE: 1.2 miles

TRAIL MAINTENANCE VOLUNTEERS

Is the trail too muddy for your tastes? Are more boardwalks needed? Is there a newly fallen tree that needs to be cut? The Superior Hiking Trail is maintained by us, the trail users. If you or your group would like to lend a helping hand, let us know. Contact the SHTA to volunteer.

4.5 (1.2)
WEST JUNCTION OF LEVEAUX MTN. SPUR TRAIL

Spur trail goes to top of Leveaux Mtn. for several typical grand Lake overlooks, also spur trail to Cobblestone Cabins and Chateau Leveaux. The west end of spur trail is steeper, rougher than east end. Leveaux Mtn. spur trail rejoins SHT at 4.7 (1.0).

5.1 (0.6)
BRIDGE ACROSS ONION RIVER

Campsite 0.1 miles past river.

▲ ONION RIVER CAMPSITE

TYPE: Multi-group
TENT PADS: 8
WATER: From Onion River
SETTING: 0.5 mile from Forest Rd.
   336, high above Onion River
PREVIOUS CAMPSITE: 1.2 miles
NEXT CAMPSITE: 2.0 miles

5.7 (0.0)
OBERG MTN. TRAILHEAD

LUTSEN-TOFTE TOURISM ASSOCIATION

Imagine having the task of promoting and marketing tourism in an area that is rich with rugged, beautiful landscapes featuring the largest body of freshwater in the world. Throw in recreational opportunities for all seasons. That is the job of the Lutsen-Tofte Tourism Association (LTTA). This organization includes most of the lodging accommodations from Little Marais to just east of the Cascade River. The participating businesses in this area offer a wide variety of accommodations from rustic to luxurious, and dining options range from a shore lunch picnic to white linen table cloths. The LTTA also offers lodge-to-lodge hiking packages along the SHT, allowing hikers to enjoy the best of both worlds; wilderness hiking as a backpacker would experience during the day, followed by fine lodging and meals during the night. Many resorts also offer shuttle service to trailheads and route information for their guests.

Oberg Mountain to Lutsen

START (END)
Oberg Mtn. parking lot on Forest Rd. 336 (Onion River Rd.)

END (START)
Lutsen Ski Area, on Cook Co. Rd. 5 (Ski Hill Rd.)

LENGTH OF TRAIL SECTION
7.0 miles

SAFETY CONCERNS
• Steep overlooks on Oberg Mtn.

• Steep slopes on both sides of Moose Mtn.

ACCESS AND PARKING
Nearest Hwy. 61 milepost: 87.5

Secondary road name and number: Forest Rd. 336 (Onion River Rd.)

Etc: Turnoff is marked by SHT sign and XC ski sign, but is easy to miss otherwise. Go north on Forest Rd. 336 approximately 2.2 miles to parking area on left side of road, opposite of Oberg trailhead. 30 spaces available. Overnight okay.

FACILITIES
At starting trailhead (farthest southwest): outhouse

Designated campsites on this section of the SHT: three

SYNOPSIS
This section has a bit of everything, from the scenic overlooks of Oberg Mtn. and Moose Mtn. to the dense maple forests of the east end. After the optional climb to Oberg Mtn., the SHT winds through boreal forests of birch, spruce, balsam fir, and alder then climbs to the top of Moose Mtn., where the views in all directions are rewarding. The ups and downs make this one of the more challenging sections. The last three miles go through a rich maple forest before emerging at the gorge of the Poplar River. This section was constructed by the Forest Service and is one of the oldest sections of the SHT.

OBERG LOOP

This is a 1.8 mile loop around the summit of Oberg Mtn. Oberg is covered by a rich maple forest, which gives out only at the many scenic overlooks. Work your way counterclockwise around the summit for about eight different overlooks in all directions, starting with Leveaux Mtn. and the Lake (and a distant Carlton Peak), then Moose Mtn., and finally inland to Oberg Lake and the rolling crests of inland ridges. Trail is well-maintained and overlooks are developed for safety. One of the overlooks has a picnic table. This is a great hike any time of year, but especially in the fall when the colors of this mountain and Leveaux Mtn. are at their peak.

MILE-BY-MILE DESCRIPTION

0.0 (7.0)
OBERG MTN. PARKING LOT

SHT leaves from opposite side of Forest Rd. 336, up some wooden steps. Trailhead is marked both by SHT sign and "National Recreation Trail" sign. Junction of Oberg Mtn. loop at 0.2 miles, a great side trip of about 1.8 miles (see sidebar). Follow SHT at junction, as indicated by the sign. SHT continues clockwise around the base of Oberg Mtn., through dense shrubs. Oberg Lake visible through trees to the north. SHT descends into wet area then crosses a creek.

1.2 (5.8)
JUNCTION WITH XC TRAIL

SHT goes straight across XC trail and also snowmobile trail. Mixed forest, with tall quaking aspen, a huge cedar tree, and lots of bluebead lily. At one point in this stretch you can see Oberg Mtn. and pick out the shape of a human face high in the rock wall. Throughout this section the SHT is marked by white diamonds as well as the SHT sign. Just before Rollins Creek, spur to campsite.

▲ WEST ROLLINS CREEK CAMPSITE

TYPE: Regular
TENT PADS: 5
WATER: From Rollins Creek
SETTING: 1.6 miles east of Forest Rd. 336, in a large cedar grove
PREVIOUS CAMPSITE: 2.0 miles
NEXT CAMPSITE: 0.1 mile

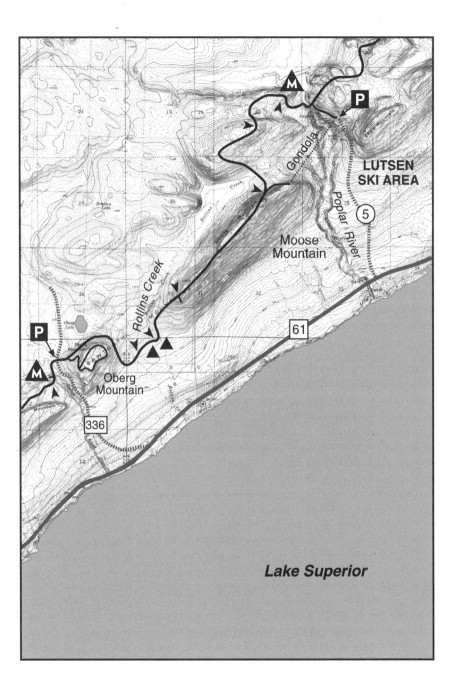

Lake Superior

1.6 (5.4)
PLANK BRIDGE OVER ROLLINS CREEK

SHT follows creek upstream a ways, then ascends from valley up flank of Moose Mtn., through yellow birch, cedar, and spruce, then paper birch, aspen, and fir. SHT gets steeper and steeper. Look for northern plants like shinleaf pyrola and twinflower near switchbacks on south side of Moose Mtn.

▲ **EAST ROLLINS CREEK CAMPSITE**

TYPE: Regular
TENT PADS: 4
WATER: From Rollins Creek
SETTING: 1.7 miles east of Forest Rd. 336
PREVIOUS CAMPSITE: 0.1 mile
NEXT CAMPSITE: 4.5 miles

2.2 (4.8)
SOUTHWEST END OF MOOSE MTN. RIDGETOP

Short, unmaintained spur to partial overlook of Lake, Oberg Mtn. Moose Mtn. is 1688 feet above sea level and 1086 feet above the Lake. SHT winds along ridgetop, with partial views on both sides. Forest here is quite northern in composition, with spruce, birch, and balsam fir, and little undergrowth. Listen for the chatter of red squirrels. Maples only in low areas.

3.4 (3.6)
SPUR TO GONDOLA

0.8 mile spur to northeast end of Moose Mtn., to Lutsen ski area gondola terminal and good views. A popular day excursion is to take the gondola to the top of Moose Mtn. and then hike the SHT back to the chalet, a total of 3.5 miles. SHT descends along north side of Moose Mtn. Descent is steep and rugged, with large basaltic outcroppings and a dark, shaded forest. SHT continues north, across plank bridge (headwaters of Rollins Creek, which SHT also crosses 1.5 miles to the SW), and enters thick, regenerating maple forest. Note all ages of maple trees, from seedling to mature. SHT slowly climbs.

5.2 (1.8)
OVERLOOK
Small, unmarked overlook off side of SHT on Lutsen ski hills, gondola, and down Poplar River valley to Lake. SHT continues in maples, then forest changes to birch and spruce. 400 yards before campsite, there is a spur to overlook marked by sign—to views of Poplar River valley.

6.1 (0.9)
CAMPSITE
Campsite is just off SHT. Just past campsite is 10-yard spur to overlook over marshy Poplar River, spruce swamp. SHT descends into wet area with scrubby alders, birches, thimbleberries, and raspberries. SHT turns onto XC ski trail (jct. marked by SHTA sign). SHT follows Poplar River gorge on wide trailbed, then crosses river on a wide bridge over a spectacular waterfall. Spur to parking lot goes downstream, SHT goes upstream on to Caribou Trail. Follow spur 0.1 mile to junction with dirt road, then another 0.3 mile to parking lot at Lutsen Ski hill.

⚠ MYSTERY MOUNTAIN CAMPSITE
TYPE: Multi-group
TENT PADS: 8
WATER: 0.5 mile away at Poplar River
SETTING: 1.0 mile to Co. Rd. 5, overlooking Poplar River Valley
PREVIOUS CAMPSITE: 4.5 miles
NEXT CAMPSITE: 1.9 miles

7.0 (0.0)
LUTSEN SKI AREA PARKING LOT
Parking lot is adjacent to Gondola terminal.

Lutsen to Caribou Trail

START (END)
Lutsen ski area, on Cook Co. Rd. 5 (Ski Hill Rd.)

END (START)
Cook Co. Rd. 4 (Caribou Trail) north of town of Lutsen

LENGTH OF TRAIL SECTION
6.4 miles

ACCESS AND PARKING
Nearest Hwy. 61 milepost: 90.1

Secondary road name and number: Cook Co. Rd. 5 (Ski Hill Rd.)

Etc: Go 2.9 miles to end of road, past Alpine Slide, chalet and gondola terminal. Parking for 8–10 cars. Overnight okay.

FACILITIES
At starting trailhead (farthest southwest): bathrooms, telephone, drinking water

Designated campsites on this section of the SHT: four

SYNOPSIS
This is a very pleasant and interesting segment of the SHT, with a diverse forest ranging from a mature maple canopy through mixed birch/aspen/pine and spruce to a small clear-cut. Stretches parallel the Poplar River and Lake Agnes, and there are several open vistas of the Poplar River drainage. In late summer it is a mushroom-hunter's heaven in terms of variety and supply.

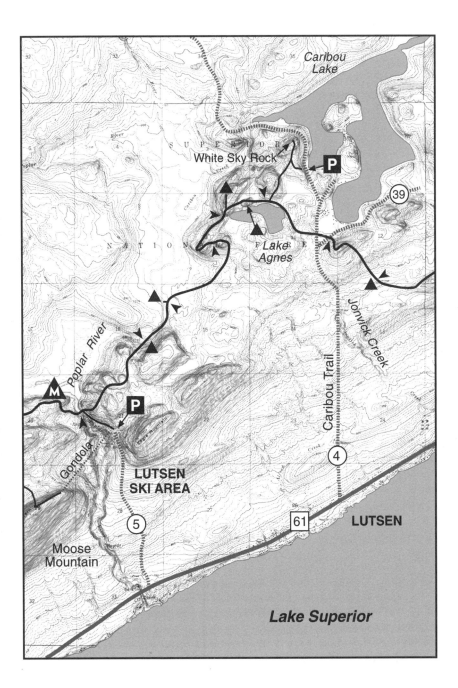

Caribou Lake

White Sky Rock

P

39

Lake Agnes

Jonvick Creek

Poplar River

M

Caribou Trail

P

4

LUTSEN SKI AREA

Gondola

5

61

LUTSEN

Moose Mountain

Lake Superior

MILE-BY-MILE DESCRIPTION

0.0 (6.4)
TRAILHEAD FOR SPUR
Follow spur trail along old Co. Rd. 5 through mixed forest. Spur forks off old road to left. The spur soon meets the SHT by the wide bridge across Poplar River. SHT winds northeast through switchbacks to overlook on ski area. SHT then enters mature maple forest and gently rolling terrain. The SHT crosses a ski/bike trail, then continues to Glove Overlook, a rock outcrop with views north and west on Poplar River valley. This area was the site of the 1990 Rainbow Gathering. SHT winds down through pine and aspen forest.

1.5 (4.9)
POPLAR RIVER WEST CAMPSITE
SHT follows river after campsite, crosses a snowmobile trail at 2.0 miles, which has a bridge over the river. This area is heavily travelled by moose, so keep an eye out for tracks, antler rubs, and huge brown deer.

▲ WEST POPLAR RIVER CAMPSITE

TYPE: Regular
TENT PADS: 4
WATER: From Poplar River
SETTING: 1.5 miles east of Lutsen, on the river
PREVIOUS CAMPSITE: 2.1 miles
NEXT CAMPSITE: 0.6 mile

2.1 (4.3)
POPLAR RIVER EAST CAMPSITE
Lots of moose sign. Mostly spruce swamp for 1/4 mile, with SHT crossing many log footbridges. SHT leaves low area and ascends past small clearcut and into mature forest.

▲ EAST POPLAR RIVER CAMPSITE

TYPE: Regular
TENT PADS: 4
WATER: From Poplar River
SETTING: 2.1 miles east of Lutsen, on the river
PREVIOUS CAMPSITE: 0.6 mile
NEXT CAMPSITE: 3.0 mile

4.0 (2.4)
OVERLOOK ON POPLAR RIVER
First of three overlooks on Poplar River valley. All three are good lunch break spots, with views of valley and river snaking far below, also of Lake. Mature maple forest.

5.0 (1.4)
AGNES CREEK BRIDGE
Bridge built in 1989; note beaver dam. SHT climbs steeply to Lake Agnes overlook, with its trail register for hikers' entries. SHT descends to lakeshore and very nice campsite on lake.

▲ WEST LAKE AGNES CAMPSITE

TYPE: Regular
TENT PADS: 4
WATER: From Lake Agnes
SETTING: 1.3 miles west of Caribou Trail,
   in maple grove overlooking Lake Agnes
PREVIOUS CAMPSITE: 3.0 miles
NEXT CAMPSITE: 0.3 mile

▲ EAST LAKE AGNES CAMPSITE

TYPE: Regular
TENT PADS: 4
WATER: From Lake Agnes
SETTING: 1.0 mile to Caribou Trail, right on lake
PREVIOUS CAMPSITE: 0.3 mile
NEXT CAMPSITE: 2.4 miles

5.6 (0.8)
SPUR TRAIL TO PARKING LOT
Sign clearly marks directions and mileage.

• Spur trail away from Lake Agnes 0.9 miles to Caribou Trail parking lot, past Cedar Hill, through a narrow rock canyon where a staircase has been sculpted from a single log, across a snowmobile trail, and up to White Sky Rock, overlooking Caribou Lake. Descend from there to parking lot.

**ECOLOGY OF NORTH AND
SOUTH SLOPES**

Many factors lead to the particular kind of trees and other plants at any given point along the trail. One factor that is often apparent along the trail is the difference between north- and south-facing slopes. Experienced hikers know the old wisdom that moss grows on the north side of trees. The same holds true for the ridgelines of the North Shore. Along the ridgeline, the forest on the southern or Lake side receives significantly more sunshine than the forest on the northern, inland side. This added sunshine makes the forest warmer and drier, an environment friendly to trees of the northern hardwood type, such as birch, aspen, oak, and maple. The cooler, moister north-facing slopes have, in general, a more boreal feel, with spruces and fir, as well as the proverbial moss. Keep an eye out for these subtle changes!

• SHT crosses XC trail, Lake Agnes access road, one more XC trail, one more snowmobile trail, and then goes through open forest and maples.

**6.4 (0.0)
CARIBOU TRAIL**

Caribou Trail to
Cascade River State Park

START (END)
Cook Co. Rd. 4 (Caribou Trail)

END (START)
Cascade River State Park, on
Hwy. 61

LENGTH OF TRAIL SECTION
9.4 miles

SAFETY CONCERNS
- Crossing beaver dam at
  Jonvick Creek is tricky—would
  recommend use of hiking stick
  when crossing. Boardwalk constructed on top of dam.

ACCESS AND PARKING
Nearest Hwy. 61 milepost: 92

Secondary road name and number: Cook Co. Rd. 4 (Caribou
Trail). Parking lot is 4.1 miles up
Caribou Trail (SHT crosses at
3.1 miles). Room for 5-6 cars.
This is also a public boat landing
for Caribou Lake. There are two
ways to access the main SHT.

SPUR TRAIL
From parking area cross Caribou
Trail and follow spur trail 0.9
mile back toward White Sky
Rock and Lake Agnes.

ROAD WALK
Walk 1 mile down Caribou Trail
to place where SHT crosses.

FACILITIES
At starting trailhead (farthest
southwest): outhouses at Caribou
Lake boat landing

Designated campsites on this section of the SHT: three

SYNOPSIS
This section follows along ridgelines with many views of Lake
and inland ridges of Sawtooth
range. The variety of habitats is
as broad as anywhere on the
SHT, with everything from
mature maple forests to dense
groves of cedar, from a massive
beaver pond to wide-open hillsides. It begins with a moderately
steep ascent but drops gently to a
valley and crosses a beaver dam.
It crosses two scenic creeks and
enters into the west end of
Cascade State Park.

MILE-BY-MILE DESCRIPTION

0.0 (9.4)
CARIBOU TRAIL

SHT crosses ditch, past some corduroy and wet spots, and the climbing wall of the Cathedral of the Pines camp. Cross Co. Rd. 39. This land all belongs to the camp, so please no camping or fires. Moderate to steep climb through big cedar and maple to ridge with vista at left of Caribou Lake. Two log benches are available for sitting and viewing lake. Many trails which are part of the camp intermingle with SHT. At 0.4 miles in, SHT turns down gentle slope through maple forest. Maples turn to alder thicket as SHT approaches Jonvick Creek and crosses some small plank bridges. Watch for woodcock near pond.

▲ JONVICK CREEK CAMPSITE

TYPE: Regular
TENT PADS: 4
WATER: From beaver pond—treat before using
SETTING: 1.4 miles east of Caribou Trail, on active beaver pond
PREVIOUS CAMPSITE: 2.4 miles
NEXT CAMPSITE: 2.2 miles

1.4 (8.0)
JONVICK CREEK CROSSING

Beavers have built a dam at crossing site. You can cross on the boardwalk built on top of dam. Consider use of hiking stick for balance. Immediately after dam, SHT crosses a wide, grassy snowmobile trail, then meanders through aspen. SHT crosses XC trail from Solbakken Resort, then rises up gentle slope through mature aspen to maple grove and views of Lake on top of ridge. SHT follows open area of young spruce (a Forest Service plantation) with wide views of Lake, crossing two dirt roads (one called the Hall Rd.), then reenters maples. SHT continues along ridgeline in cedar and pine, with views of inland ridges, then descends. As with other ridges on the SHT, hawks are visible from this ridge during fall migration.

3.6 (5.8)
SPRUCE CREEK CROSSING
Campsite on east side of bridge. SHT continues up through white pines and maples, across a snowmobile trail to another ridgeline with views of Lake and inland ridges, then slopes down to an open, sometimes muddy area and back up to another ridgeline with almost pure maple.

⚠ SPRUCE CREEK CAMPSITE

TYPE: Multi-group
TENT PADS: 8
WATER: From Spruce Creek
SETTING: 3.6 miles east of
  Caribou Trail
PREVIOUS CAMPSITE: 2.2 miles
NEXT CAMPSITE: 3.3 miles

5.2 (4.2)
JUNCTION WITH SNOWMOBILE TRAIL
SHT uses wider snowmobile trail for 0.5 miles, continuing up and down along grassy, open narrow ridge. Watch carefully as SHT leaves snowmobile trail sharply to left, then climbs ridge to view of inland ridges and the lakeshore toward Grand Marais, before descending along curving ridgeline and cliff edge, past 10-yard spur to viewpoint.

CASCADE RIVER STATE PARK

Named for the series of stair-stepping waterfalls on the Cascade River, Cascade River State Park offers numerous spectacular views along trails and bridges that follow and cross the river. Its 2813 acres follow a half-mile-wide band along 1-1/2 miles of Lake Superior shoreline. Cascade served as an Emergency Conservation Work (ECW) camp during the 1930's. Their handi-work includes the trails that follow the river. Within the park are eighteen miles of hiking trails, many of which connect with the Superior Hiking Trail and other trails in the Superior National Forest. Located within the park is an enclosed picnic shelter, a modern campground with 40 drive-in sites, two group camp sites, and five backpack sites, one located on the Lake Superior shore. A small picnic area is also located along the Lake.

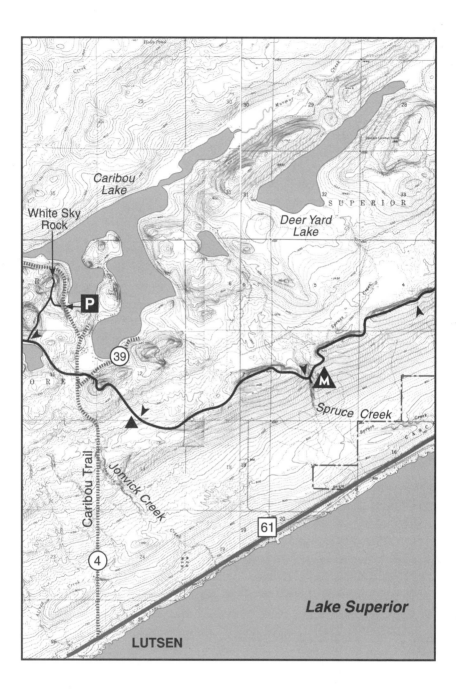

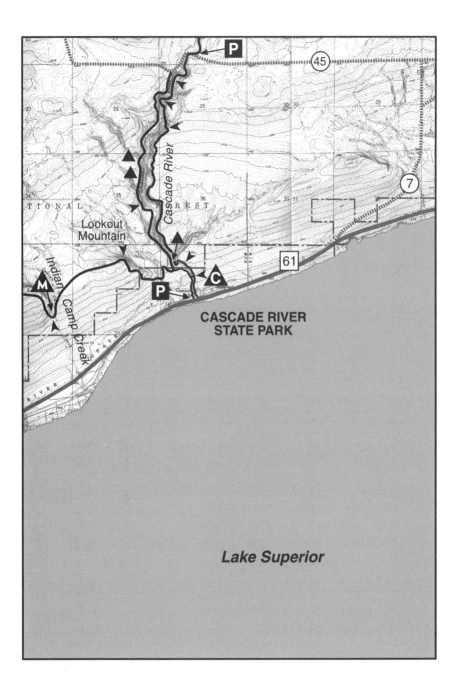

**CASCADE RIVER
STATE PARK**

Lake Superior

6.9 (2.5)
INDIAN CAMP CREEK

Campsite on east side of creek. SHT crosses a snowmobile trail, meanders through woods of cedar, pine and aspen, then down to wooden walkways across potentially muddy springs. Downed and dying fir are victims of spruce budworm infestation. SHT then climbs through aspen woods, meets state park XC trail and follows this trail past a state park trail map to junction with shelter, picnic table and outhouse. SHT forks off XC trail and heads up.

⚠ INDIAN CAMP CREEK CAMPSITE

TYPE: Multi-group
TENT PADS: 8
WATER: From Indian Camp Creek
SETTING: 2.5 miles west of Cascade River State Park
PREVIOUS CAMPSITE: 3.3 miles
NEXT CAMPSITE: 3.3 miles if following west side of Cascade River; 3.2 miles if
    following east side of Cascade River (or use Cascade River State Park)

8.1 (1.3)
LOOKOUT MTN.

Benches and a trail register at overlook. SHT stays left and descends, crossing XC trail to Cascade Lodge. SHT passes large stumps left over from white pine logging, then crosses another XC trail. Wooden plank crosses a small feeder stream, and then SHT joins Cascade River State Park trail. SHT turns (left) onto XC trail soon after crossing stream, following State Park "Hiking Club" signs. Watch for signed trail junction at top of the famous "96 steps." This is one end of the Cascade River loop trail. Don't turn here, though, unless you want to miss the great views of one of the most photographed series of North Shore waterfalls. At the bridge over the river there is a platform for viewing the falls.

9.2 (0.2)
CASCADE RIVER BRIDGE

The spur trails to the Hwy. 61 parking lot go directly from the bridge down either side of the river.

9.4 (0.0)
CASCADE RIVER PARKING LOT

Cascade River State Park to Bally Creek Road

START (END)
Parking lot on inland side Hwy. 61 in Cascade State Park

END (START)
Forest Rd. 158 (Bally Creek Rd.)

LENGTH OF TRAIL SECTION
9.5 miles using east side of river; 9.5 miles using west side of river

SAFETY CONCERNS
• Several steeper slopes can be slippery when wet, particularly on descents

ACCESS AND PARKING
HWY. 61 TRAILHEAD
Nearest Hwy. 61 milepost: 99.9

Secondary road name and number: none

Etc: Two parking options:

1) Park on north side of Hwy. 61, just southwest of Cascade River bridge. 8 spaces on Hwy. 61, 6 hour limit.

2) For longer or overnight parking, use the 2 small lots next to the shelter in the campground. There is a second trailhead here. Ask ranger for permission. State Park permit required.

ACCESS AND PARKING:
COOK CO. RD. 45 TRAILHEAD
Nearest Hwy. 61 milepost: 101.5

Secondary road name and number: go 2.0 miles on Co. Rd. 7 (Pike Lake Rd.), left on Co. Rd. 44 for 0.5 miles, left on Co. Rd. 45 for 2.6 miles.

Etc. Park on right just before bridge. Lot holds 12 cars. Overnight okay

FACILITIES
At starting trailhead: bathrooms, outhouses, telephone, drinking water (all in state park facilities)

Designated campsites on this section of the SHT: five

SYNOPSIS
After ascending the scenic Cascade River valley, this section of the SHT enters a long, remote area. The Hidden Falls section is a highlight, as well as the remote woods and tree plantations east of Co. Rd. 45.

The 7.8 mile Cascade River loop is a popular daytrip, up one side of the river and down the other.

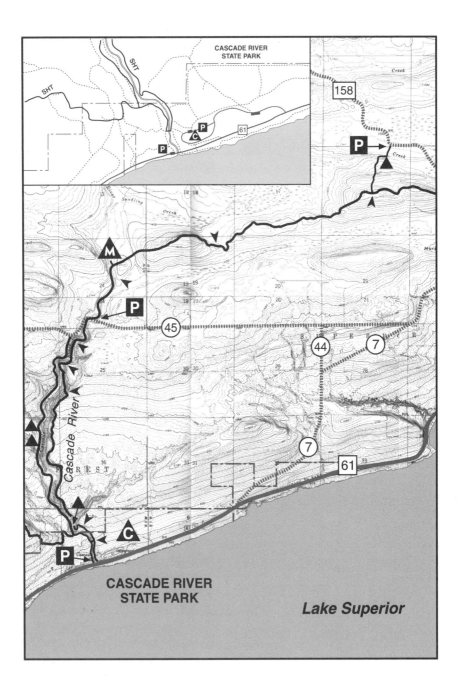

CASCADE RIVER STATE PARK

CASCADE RIVER STATE PARK

STATE PARK

Lake Superior

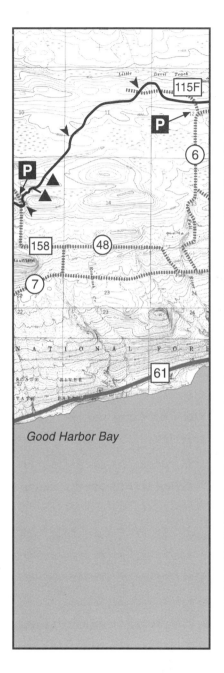

Good Harbor Bay

GEOLOGY OF NORTH SHORE WATERFALLS

The North Shore is blessed by many beautiful waterfalls, including several that give the name to the Cascade River. The abundance of waterfalls is basically the result of two factors: 1) the profound erosion of the Lake Superior basin by the great Ice Age glaciers, which led to the steep slope of the North Shore; and 2) the occurrence of hard igneous rocks underlying the coastal zone. The fast-running rivers have eroded the softer bedrock to form the deeper parts of the gorges. However, the bedrock has some harder parts, such as dikes or the lower parts of lava flows, and these resist erosion, leading to falls and cascades. Many of the falls on the Cascade River represent individual basalt lava flows.

MILE-BY-MILE DESCRIPTION

0.0 (9.5)
TRAILHEAD
Directly north of the Hwy. 61 bridge over the Cascade River, behind the guard rail. This is a spur trail and there is no SHT marker. Spur trail climbs up steps. Look for Cascade Falls below.

0.2 (9.3)
FOOTBRIDGE AT FALLS SHT SPLIT
At this point SHT goes up either the west or east banks of the Cascade River. This is a popular long loop hike up one side and down the other.

FOLLOWING WEST SIDE OF CASCADE RIVER
From footbridge over falls climb along ski trails to the "96 steps," an ambitious bit of engineering that brings the SHT down to the river side above the cascades. Like most North Shore streams, this rather gentle river becomes the famed cascades only as it passes through bedrock downstream.

1.4 (8.1)
SPUR TRAIL TO "SECRET WATERFALL"
Spur runs 0.3 mile to the "secret waterfall." 0.2 mile past spur, SHT passes an old mine site. There is an old shaft on the right side of trail which is now full of water, and the remains of some building foundations on the trailside. SHT then crosses bridge over tributary of the Cascade River.

▲ BIG WHITE PINE CAMPSITE

TYPE: Regular
TENT PADS: 4
WATER: From small creek
SETTING: 1.6 miles from Cascade River State Park
PREVIOUS CAMPSITE: 3.3 miles (or use State Park)
NEXT CAMPSITE: 0.5 mile

2.3 (7.2)
CUT LOG CAMPSITE
After crossing a 25-foot bridge you come to the Cut Log Campsite. Check out the remains of two very large white pines cut by loggers many years ago and left behind. One of these logs, at the edge of the campsite, is nearly 4 feet in diameter. SHT continues through the valley of a tributary. Catch some outstanding views of the Cascade River just before the SHT intersects Co. Rd. 45

▲ CUT LOG CAMPSITE

TYPE: Regular
TENT PADS: 4
WATER: From small creek below campsite
SETTING: 2.1 miles from Cascade River State Park
PREVIOUS CAMPSITE: 0.5 mile
NEXT CAMPSITE: 2.3 miles

3.6 (5.9)
JUNCTION WITH CO. RD. 45
Follow Co. Rd. 0.3 mile to junction with east side trail at parking lot. This ends west side trail. Hikers can now either return to Hwy. 61 on the east side going downstream (right turn) or go on to Bally Creek going upstream (left side)

FOLLOWING EAST SIDE CASCADE RIVER
SHT crosses bridge above gorgeous waterfalls and meets a spur from the state park trailhead and campground. SHT climbs steeply, then levels off. SHT soon turns off of state park hiking/ski trail. At this point, look for short spur to an overlook of the river. SHT descends Trout Creek, crosses bridge and passes campsite to left.

1.3 (8.2)
CAMPSITE ENTRANCE
SHT soon enters private land, as marked by sign. Be respectful of the owners' rights and do not camp, light fires, or go off SHT. SHT follows bluff above river, with occasional views and sounds of the river below. Note how tree mix along river differs from that along bluff.

▲ TROUT CREEK CAMPSITE

TYPE: Regular
TENT PADS: 5
WATER: From Cascade River
SETTING: 1.1 miles from Highway 61, on steep river bank
PREVIOUS CAMPSITE: 3.2 miles
NEXT CAMPSITE: 3.7 miles

3.2 (6.3)
SHT RETURNS TO RIVER

SHT makes steep descent to river's edge, climbs partway up bluff, and makes another steep descent to river (hiking sticks may be helpful, particularly if ground is wet). Note Hidden Falls, a very picturesque area with several good rest spots. SHT departs private land as it continues along Cascade River through cedar, pine, alder and birch.

3.9 (5.6)
CO. RD. 45 AND PARKING LOT

SHT passes under bridge, into parking lot, and continues from left side of lot entrance road, about 100 feet in from Co. Rd. 45. If you're doing the Cascade River loop, walk 0.3 miles west (left, across the bridge) on Co. Rd. 45 to the next trailhead. This area had a CCC camp in the early 1930s. SHT leads gradually along ridge, descends to cross Minnow Trap Creek and then climbs steps to follow top of bluff along Cascade River. Note views of river and ridges to northwest.

TRAILS FROM WEST AND EAST SIDE OF RIVER JOIN

An optional parking lot is here on Co. Rd. 45. SHT continues up the river in gentler country now.

4.6 (4.9)
CAMPSITE

At campsite spur, SHT turns sharply and moves away from river. SHT climbs gradually, passing through alder thickets, across planks, and through a stand of young red pine (whose needles carpet the ground) to reach a ridge overlooking the Sundling Creek valley. Eagle Mtn., the highest point in Minnesota, is visible from here. Note views across valley to north and government survey markers with "bearing trees." SHT descends past a series of cross trails and steps to XC trail.

⛺ NORTH CASCADE RIVER CAMPSITE

TYPE: Multi-group
TENT PADS: 8
WATER: From Cascade River
SETTING: 0.7 mile north of Co. Rd. 45
PREVIOUS CAMPSITE: 2.3 miles on west side of Cascade River or 3.7 miles on east side of Cascade River
NEXT CAMPSITE: 4.3 miles

6.0 (3.5)
CROSS XC SKI TRAIL

SHT climbs low ridge and follows edge of logged area. Note rapid aspen growth as the quick-growing tree sprouts from runners. SHT then climbs another ridge with views back to Lake. SHT continues along several ridges though mixed forest to a high point on the ridge.

8.4 (1.1)
SPUR TRAIL

Spur goes north to Bally Creek Rd. (Forest Rd. 158) parking lot. Spur trail leads 0.7 mile to parking lot. Spur goes through birch forest, crosses a low area, climbs a low ridge and descends to beaver pond on Sundling Creek. Beaver dam is visible from spur trail—ignore beavers' cross trails. Spur crosses creek, then follows a rise into parking lot.

▲ SUNDLING CREEK CAMPSITE

TYPE: Regular
TENT PADS: 4
WATER: From Sundling Creek
SETTING: 0.2 mile from Bally Creek Rd. parking lot on spur trail
PREVIOUS CAMPSITE: 4.3 miles
NEXT CAMPSITE: 1.7 miles

SHT continues along ridgeline through hardwoods with many views to north. SHT begins gradual descent through stand of young red pine, then descends to Bally Creek Rd. (Forest Rd. 158).

9.5 (0.0)
BALLY CREEK RD.

Bally Creek Road to Grand Marais

START (END)
Forest Rd. 158 (Bally Creek Rd.)

END (START)
Pincushion Mt. trailhead north of Grand Marais, Co. Rd. 53 (Pincushion Dr.)

LENGTH OF TRAIL SECTION
8.3 miles

SAFETY CONCERNS
• Cliffs on Sawtooth Bluff

• Gunflint Trail crossing

ACCESS AND PARKING
BALLY CREEK ROAD
Nearest Hwy. 61 milepost: 101.7

Secondary Road name and number: Co. Rd. 7

Follow Co. Rd. 7 approximately 4.3 miles to a dirt road (Co. Rd. 48), then left for 0.3 miles to "T" intersection with Forest Rd. 158. Left on Forest Rd. 158 for 1 mile to spot where main SHT crosses the road, parking on the left for 4-5 cars. There is additional parking 1.5 miles farther along Forest Rd. 158, 10–15 parking spaces available.

ACCESS AND PARKING
COOK CO. RD. 6
Nearest Hwy 61 milepost: 101.7

Etc: Follow Co. Rd. 7, 6.0 miles to Co. Rd. 6. Left on Co. Rd. 6 1.5 miles to parking area at intersection of Forest Rd. 115F.

FACILITIES
At starting trailhead: none

Designated campsites on this section of the SHT: Two

SYNOPSIS
This is one of the newest sections of the SHT. The western half of this section is marked by a large beaver pond and Sundling Creek. The SHT passes through a large red pine forest before it joins the North Shore State Trail for 2 miles. Near Grand Marais the trail visits Sawtooth Bluff, with its beautiful vistas of Lake Superior. From west to east this is a particularly nice walk for novice hikers ready for a longer trek.

MILE-BY-MILE DESCRIPTION

0.0 (8.3)
JUNCTION WITH BALLY CREEK ROAD

The first campsite spur is only 0.1 mile into the hike.

▲ SOUTH BALLY CREEK POND CAMPSITE

TYPE: Regular
TENT PADS: 4
WATER: From beaver pond—treat before using
SETTING: 0.2 mile from Bally Creek Rd., on pristine beaver pond
PREVIOUS CAMPSITE: 1.7 miles
NEXT CAMPSITE: 0.2 miles

SHT crosses a 13' bridge over a small creek that drains the beaver pond and skirts the beaver pond.

▲ NORTH BALLY CREEK POND CAMPSITE

TYPE: Regular
TENT PADS: 4
WATER: From beaver pond—treat before using
SETTING: 0.3 mile from Bally Creek Rd., on pristine beaver pond
PREVIOUS CAMPSITE: 0.2 miles
NEXT CAMPSITE: 10.5 miles

There is a short climb away from the pond into mixed deciduous forest then a gradual descent to Sundling Creek through pines. Find a rest bench to the right at Sundling Creek.

0.8 (7.5)
SUNDLING CREEK DAM

193' of boardwalk over the creek with a nice view of the creek upstream. Next ascend back into mixed conifers and aspen. SHT passes through a cluster of 9 birch trees. A wet area follows with a 15' bridge over a small creek. Then SHT exits the deep forest and enters a cut-over area with many young trees evident.

2.1 (6.2)
WEST CROSSING OF USFS 115F

SHT crosses this old forest road three times within a mile. SHT soon enters one of the largest red pine forests on the entire length of the

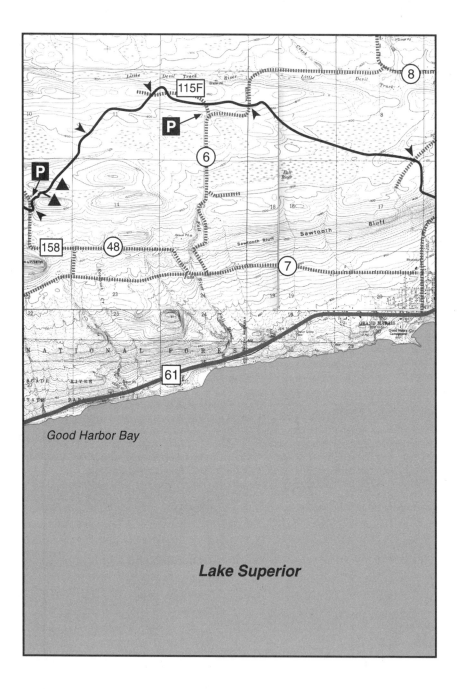

Good Harbor Bay

Lake Superior

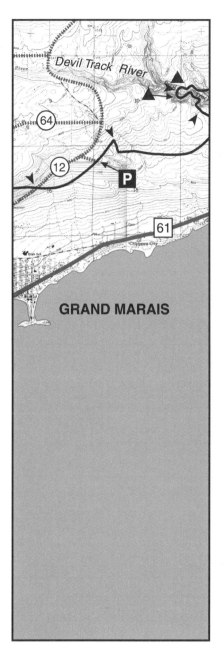

trail, a plantation planted in 1937. Look for moose in this area, as trail builders and early users of this section observed both bulls and cows.

At the easterly of the three crossings, at 3.1(5.2), a spur trail heads 0.1 mile south to Cook Co. Rd. 6 and parking lot. SHT continues east with more of the red pine forest.

3.7 (4.6)
COOK CO. RD. 6 CROSSING
SHT crosses the road and continues 0.2 mile to the North Shore State Trail. SHT follows the North Shore State Trail for the next 2.5 miles. The North Shore State Trail is a wider path used by snowmobiles and the John Beargrease Sled Dog Race in the winter. The joined trails pass through patches of young scotch pines by a very wet area and a gradual rise to a drier area bordered by mixed forest.

6.3 (2.0)
COOK CO. RD. 64
(TOWER RD.)
The radio and television transmitters are visible to the right. Shortly SHT leaves the North Shore State Trail and heads directly toward Grand Marais with Lake Superior gradually becoming visible. SHT traverses a long wet area on boardwalk. As SHT descends, the Lake becomes more vis-

ible. The SHT continues east with a very steep descent and views of Lake Superior.

7.3 (1.0)
CROSS GUNFLINT TRAIL
No parking here, but road edge is wide and safe. This is the closest access to Grand Marais for services. SHT continues on other side and goes uphill, eventually joining a XC ski trail. Continue uphill (downhill leads to High School football field), across North Shore State Trail to the dramatic views of the Pincushion Mountain trailhead.

8.3 (0.0)
PINCUSHION MTN. TRAILHEAD

Grand Marais to Cook County Road 58

START (END)
Pincushion Mountain area trailhead, on Co. Rd. 53 (Pincushion Dr.) just off Gunflint Trail

END (START)
Cook Co. Rd. 58 (Lindskog Rd.), north of Hwy. 61

LENGTH OF TRAIL SECTION
4.9 miles

SAFETY CONCERNS
• Cliffs close to trail edge at Devil Track Canyon

ACCESS AND PARKING
Nearest Hwy. 61 milepost: 109.3

Secondary road name and number: Gunflint Trail, Co. Rd. 12

Etc: Go north on Gunflint Trail 1.7 miles, then turn east on Co. Rd. 53, 1/4 mile to trailhead. Intersection at Gunflint Trail well-marked as "Scenic Overlook." 25 parking spaces. Overnight okay.

FACILITIES
At starting trailhead (farthest southwest): outhouse

Designated campsites on this section of the SHT: two

SYNOPSIS
This is a 4.9 mile walk with an optional spur to a panoramic vista from summit of Pincushion Mountain which includes the town of Grand Marais. The access to the town and services make this walk quite convenient. There are many side loops available on the Pincushion Trail system, including the overlook. Devil Track River crossing and hike on canyon edge offer dramatic views into the canyon gorge.

MILE-BY-MILE DESCRIPTION

0.0 (4.9)
PINCUSHION MOUNTAIN TRAILHEAD

This is a popular trailhead for XC skiing, with 25 kilometers of groomed trails. The SHT follows groomed trails for 2 miles. If hiking in winter, you must stay off the groomed trails unless you are using snowshoes. In that case, please stay out of the tracked section and follow the one-way directional signs. SHT passes trail junctions marked #20 and #4.

0.4 (4.5)
JUNCTION #4

SHT turns right here and goes past #19 to the spur trail to top of Pincushion Mtn. and then to the river, approximately 2.5 miles. Summit spur at 1.7 (3.2) leads 1/4 mile to summit for sweeping vistas of Grand Marais, Sawtooth Mountains and Devil Track River. Hikers are asked not to use this trail during the winter as it would take hikers in the wrong direction along the ski trails.

2.2 (2.7)
JUNCTION OF SKI TRAILS AND SHT

SHT departs ski trails and descends over 200 feet down to Devil Track River, along 150 steps installed for safety.

2.5 (2.4)
DEVIL TRACK RIVER BRIDGE

50-foot, "A"-shape bridge, built in the summer of 1992. The canyon is deep and remote. Campsites on both west and east side of river. SHT climbs uphill from campsite, about 0.2 mile to Spruce Knob, then continues along canyon's edge, crossing split log walkways at 2.9 and 3.5 miles. Watch for scenic waterfalls and gorgeous red cliffs below.

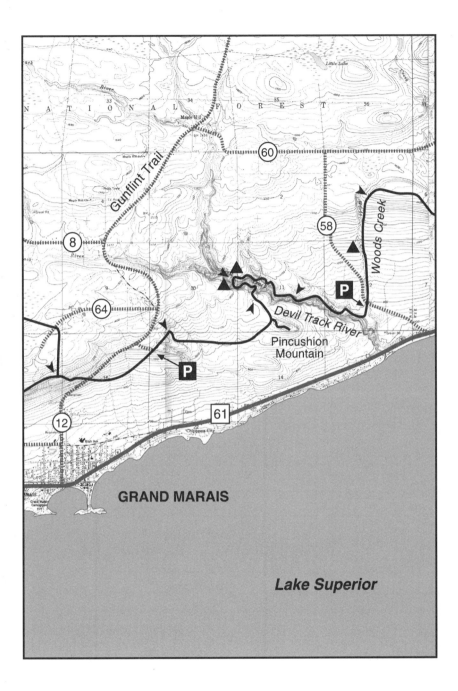

GRAND MARAIS

Lake Superior

CROSS COUNTRY SKIING & THE NORTH SHORE SNOWBELT

At numerous places, the Superior Hiking Trail intersects or shares its route with a cross-country ski trail. Ski trails are wider than the Hiking Trail, tend to be grassy, and often have blue diamonds marking their course. The winter skier can have an experience similar to that of the summer hiker, with the same beautiful forests, dramatic overlooks and ease of access. There is an extensive network of trails that link all parts of the North Shore. The winter experience is made all the more enjoyable by the generally ample snow, created by the lake-effect snowfall along the North Shore ridge-line. It's not unusual to have two feet of snow inland and none along the highway. Note: if snowshoeing the SHT in winter, please stay off of any groomed ski track.

▲ WEST DEVIL TRACK CAMPSITE

TYPE: Regular
TENT PADS: 6
WATER: From Devil Track River
SETTING: 2.5 miles from Pincushion trailhead, on west bank of river
PREVIOUS CAMPSITE: 10.5 miles
NEXT CAMPSITE: 0.1 mile

▲ EAST DEVIL TRACK CAMPSITE

TYPE: Regular
TENT PADS: 2
WATER: From Devil Track River
SETTING: 2.6 miles from Pincushion trailhead, on east bank of river
PREVIOUS CAMPSITE: 0.1 mile
NEXT CAMPSITE: 2.9 miles

3.9 (1.0)
BARRIER FALLS OVERLOOK

Deep vista into canyon. SHT passes 1937 tree plantation marker, and eventually descends cedar steps to cross small stream on bridge, which descends several vertical drops as it carves its way to the river. SHT continues through pine plantation. A fisherman's trail crosses the SHT and heads straight down to river. About 0.2 mile from parking lot is last (or first) good overlook on canyon.

4.9 (0.0)
COOK CO. RD. 58
(LINDSKOG RD.)

Cook County Road 58
to Kadunce River

START (END)
Cook Co. Rd. 58 (Lindskog Rd.)

END (START)
Kadunce River Wayside on Hwy. 61

LENGTH OF TRAIL SECTION
9.2 miles

ACCESS AND PARKING
CO. RD. 58
Nearest Hwy. 61 milepost: 113.8

Secondary road name and number: Co. Rd. 58

Etc: Go north on Co. Rd. 58 0.8 miles. Parking lot for 10 spaces. Overnight okay.

ACCESS AND PARKING
CO. RD. 14
Nearest Hwy. 61 milepost: 117.6

Secondary road name and number: Co. Rd. 14.

Etc: Go 0.7 mile from Hwy. 61. Lot holds 8 cars, overnight okay.

FACILITIES
At starting trailhead (farthest southwest): none

Designated campsites on this section of the SHT: six

SYNOPSIS
There are a number of unusual features to this section of the SHT. The section begins and ends with intimate streams, from the gentle gurgle of Wood's Creek to the deep gorges of the Kadunce River, which offer a fascinating glimpse into the region's geology. The middle part of the section takes you across a unique high, wet area with over two dozen footbridges. Unusual trees on this section include red oak and black spruce.

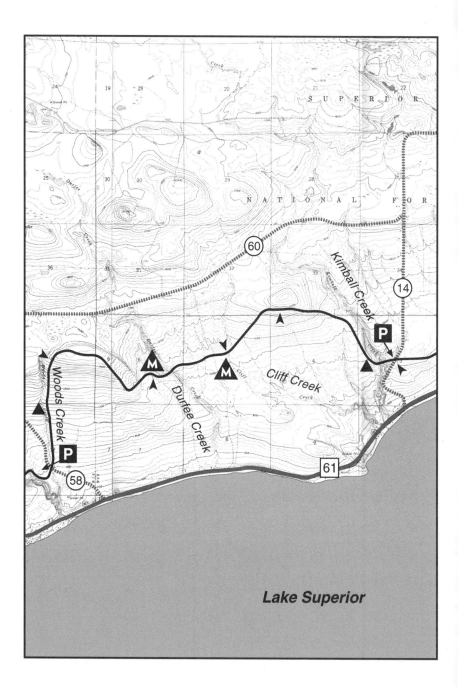

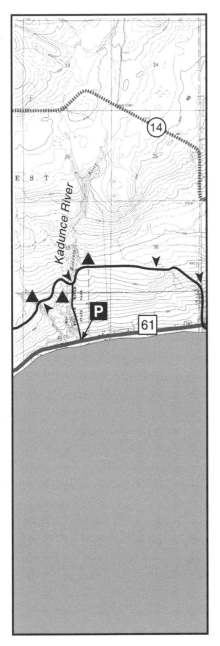

0.0 (9.2)
PARKING LOT ON CO. RD. 58

SHT begins in red pines on east side of Wood's Creek, a feeder stream to the Devil Track River, then follows bouldery stream through birch, aspen and ash. The sharp-edged red rock is rhyolite. SHT then goes through dark spruces with old man's beard (a lichen) drooping from branches.

▲ WOOD'S CREEK CAMPSITE

TYPE: Regular
TENT PADS: 4
WATER: From Woods Creek
SETTING: 0.6 mile east of
    Co. Rd. 58, on creek
PREVIOUS CAMPSITE: 2.9 miles
NEXT CAMPSITE: 2.4 miles

1.2 (8.0)
SHT LEAVES CREEK

SHT turns east and climbs into parklike birch forest, then a series of cutovers and open areas (SHT marked by rock cairns). Views of Lake, Pincushion Mtn. at first, then wide view to southwest of Pincushion, Maple Hill radio tower, and Sawtooth range. Birches gradually give way to aspens. In the open area, watch for bluebirds in the field and Five-Mile Rock in the Lake. At far side of field, SHT enters a mixed woods, crosses a trail, then passes through a wildlife opening.

3.0 (6.2)
DURFEE CREEK CAMPSITE

After campsite, SHT crosses a series of over 20 plank bridges in this up-and-down section, with lots of black spruce and burned stumps.

▲ DURFEE CREEK CAMPSITE

TYPE: Multi-group
TENT PADS: 6
WATER: From Durfee Creek
SETTING: 3.0 miles east of Co. Rd. 58
PREVIOUS CAMPSITE: 2.4 miles
NEXT CAMPSITE: 1.1 miles

4.1 (5.1)
CLIFF CREEK CROSSING

The last of the many creeks in this section. This plank is longer than the earlier ones. Now woods get more mixed, with birch, aspen and fir. Lake comes into view, maples appear, and the sharp, red rhyolite returns underfoot.

▲ CLIFF CREEK CAMPSITE

TYPE: Multi-group
TENT PADS: 8
WATER: From Cliff Creek
SETTING: 2.7 miles west of Co. Rd. 14
PREVIOUS CAMPSITE: 1.1 miles
NEXT CAMPSITE: 2.6 miles

5.1 (4.1)
SCRUB-OAK OVERLOOK

Expansive view of Lake, now including Red Cliff. On SHT look for the unusual small oak trees, then spruce plantation and large (30-inch diameter) aspens. SHT begins to follow Kimball Creek, then crosses it and meets the Kimball Creek Trail junction. SHT then crosses a tributary and climbs steep steps.

▲ KIMBALL CREEK CAMPSITE

TYPE: Regular
TENT PADS: 4
WATER: From Kimball Creek
SETTING: 0.1 mile west of
 Co. Rd. 14, at base of hill
PREVIOUS CAMPSITE: 2.6 miles
NEXT CAMPSITE: 1.2 miles

6.8 (2.4)
COOK CO. RD. 14

SHT crosses road (parking available here) and climbs through cutover area, then passes under powerline before entering a fir/birch/aspen woods. A view of Lake, then SHT descends. Look for bunchberry and thimbleberry (with galls that look like swollen kneecaps). SHT crosses a couple of footpaths and a small opening. Path is mostly rock here. SHT descends stone steps to Crow Creek.

▲ CROW CREEK CAMPSITE

TYPE: Regular
TENT PADS: 5
WATER: From Crow Creek
SETTING: 1.1 miles east of
 Co. Rd. 14
PREVIOUS CAMPSITE: 1.2 miles
NEXT CAMPSITE: 0.4 mile

UNUSUAL FORESTS

Most of Minnesota's Arrowhead is boreal forest, with typical stands of evergreen spruce and balsam fir, and deciduous birch and aspen communities. This boreal type is quite common along the SHT. Having all this similar forest makes the exceptions all the more dramatic. Watch for unusual stands of black ash, a species prized by basketmakers, in well-drained lowland areas. The high parts of the SHT wind through occasional stands of oak in the southern half, although by the time the SHT reaches Cook County, most of the oaks are gone. Other unusual tree species to watch out for include ironwood, basswood and American elm.

7.9 (1.3)
CROW CREEK

This stream has the steep rock walls typical of Kadunce River country visible upstream from the bridge. SHT climbs out of creek bed, crosses a footpath, then another narrow steep canyon, the west fork of the

PEBBLE BEACHES

A beach must have both a source of rock particles and wave action to deposit and move the particles. Beaches continually change in reaction to changes in the waves from storm to calm to storm. Some of the smaller beaches on the North Shore are made of rocks ripped from the nearby bedrock ledges; larger beaches are made possible where the waves have access to more easily-eroded glacial deposits. The long, low beaches between Grand Marais and Hovland are made both from local volcanic rhyolite, which breaks up into easily erodible chips or shingles, and reworked older beach deposits from the Nipissing stage of Lake Superior, about 5000 years ago, when the Lake was slightly higher and the beaches were on the other side of what is now the highway. Can you find any agates? They might have been brought by the ice sheet from Isle Royale or Canada.

Kadunce River. Watch for bearing tree near SHT right before crossing Kadunce River.

▲ WEST FORK OF THE KADUNCE CAMPSITE

TYPE: Regular
TENT PADS: 4
WATER: Mostly dry stream bed or Kadunce River (0.5 miles)
SETTING: 1.5 miles east of Co. Rd. 14
PREVIOUS CAMPSITE: 0.4 mile
NEXT CAMPSITE: 0.5 mile

8.5 (0.7)
KADUNCE RIVER

On far side of bridge, go downstream on spectacular spur trail to Hwy. 61. Spur follows river until river drops into gorge, then rejoins river after gorge. The river itself is a wonderful upstream hike. Hikers will get wet up to their thighs. This should be attempted only when the water is very low because four waterfalls must be ascended using all fours. The canyon is very deep yet only about 8 feet wide in places.

9.2 (0.0)
KADUNCE RIVER WAYSIDE ON HWY. 61

Kadunce River to Magney State Park

START (END)
Kadunce River Wayside on Hwy. 61

END (START)
Judge C.R. Magney State Park

LENGTH OF TRAIL SECTION
10.0 miles

SAFETY CONCERNS
- Trail near cliff edge at times along Kadunce River

ACCESS AND PARKING
KADUNCE RIVER
Nearest Hwy. 61 milepost: 119

Secondary road name and number: none

Parking spaces available: 11 spaces available, no overnight

ACCESS AND PARKING
LAKEWALK
Nearest Hwy. 61 milepost: 120.2 at west end, 121.6 at east end

Secondary road name and number: none

Parking spaces available: 6 on lakeside, no overnight

FACILITIES
At starting trailhead (farthest southwest): none

Designated campsites on this section of trail: four

SYNOPSIS
This is an exciting section of the SHT, since it is the only part which is directly on the Lake Superior shoreline. It also passes many different stages of succession following logging in the area; and some classic North Shore river gorges, including that of the Kadunce River.

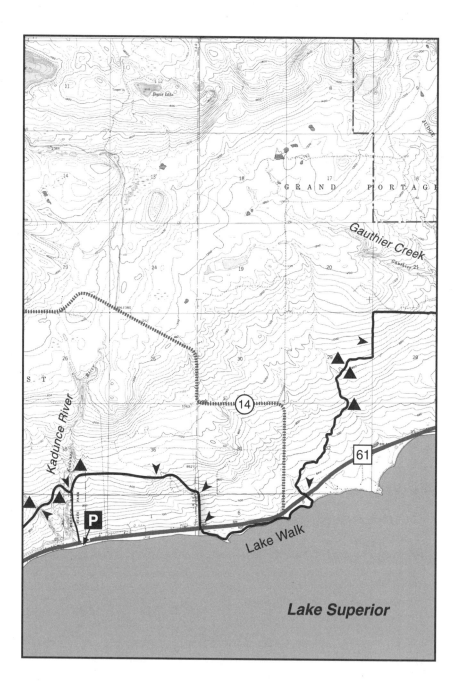

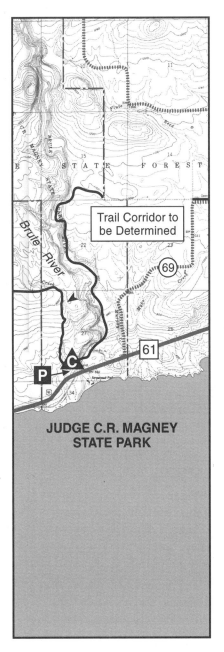

MILE-BY-MILE DESCRIPTION

0.0 (10.0)
KADUNCE WAYSIDE

This spectacular spur trail begins climbing almost immediately along the edge of the Kadunce River gorge, which is pocked by occasional "swirl caves" created at various stages of the gorge's creation. Spur begins to level out momentarily where it meets the main SHT at a bridge crossing the Kadunce River.

0.7 (9.3)
FOOTBRIDGE OVER KADUNCE RIVER

Spur trail joins main SHT here. Crossing bridge, SHT leads southwest to Co. Rd. 58. SHT turns away from bridge, then climbs hill and follows river upstream past cascades, then climbs again and leaves river. Forest changes from birch and fir to dense, relatively younger aspen stand. SHT crosses an old grassy logging roadbed and then two footpaths.

▲ **KADUNCE RIVER CAMPSITE**

TYPE: Regular
TENT PADS: 4
WATER: From Kadunce River
SETTING: 0.9 mile in from
   Hwy. 61.
PREVIOUS CAMPSITE: 0.5 mile
NEXT CAMPSITE: 5.3 miles

2.0 (8.0)
BLUEBERRY OVERLOOK
Follow rock cairns through open area which leads to overlook with expansive view of Lake Superior. SHT crosses stream and enters dark woods, then a recently logged area. Look for an old red pine stump that is a "nurse log" to a young birch. SHT then enters another logged area replanted with spruce, with large white pines left standing. SHT descends log ladder and passes many raspberry patches in a 350 acre clearcut.

2.7 (7.3)
KELLY'S HILL ROAD
SHT crosses road (note SHT mileage sign), then descends through scrubby woods, dense young aspen stand and mixed woods.

3.2 (6.8)
HWY. 61, WEST END OF LAKEWALK
SHT is marked on both sides of Hwy. 61. SHT follows shore of Lake on a soft pebble beach. This is the only part of the SHT on Lake Superior. Here one can literally touch the many moods of this great Lake. Notice the different surge levels up the beach from storms and wind, especially the unimpeded northeast winds. Look for bog areas between beach and Hwy. 61—good spring birding, as birds use shoreline for navigation. SHT turns inland just past a very small rock island barely off shore.

4.8 (5.2)
HWY. 61, EAST END OF LAKEWALK
SHT passes large birches and passes under powerline and through mixed woods along Hane Creek. Cross stream on small wood bridge after passing through low areas and logged sections. SHT eventually climbs and passes large cedar and white pine and overlooks of waterfalls and pools below. SHT crosses Little Brule River on log planking, ascends through mature aspen, then levels out. This section passes through a portion of private land. Please respect the owner's rights; stay on trail and do not camp or build fires.

▲ SOUTH LITTLE BRULE RIVER CAMPSITE

TYPE: Regular
TENT PADS: 4
WATER: From Little Brule River
SETTING: 1.5 miles from Hwy. 61
PREVIOUS CAMPSITE: 5.3 miles
NEXT CAMPSITE: 0.4 mile

▲ NORTH LITTLE BRULE RIVER CAMPSITE

TYPE: Regular
TENT PADS: 4
WATER: From Little Brule River
SETTING: 1.9 miles from Hwy. 61
PREVIOUS CAMPSITE: 0.4 mile
NEXT CAMPSITE: 0.0 mile

▲ NORTHWEST LITTLE BRULE RIVER CAMPSITE

TYPE: Regular
TENT PADS: 4
WATER: From Little Brule River
SETTING: 1.9 miles from Hwy. 61
PREVIOUS CAMPSITE: 0.0 mile
NEXT CAMPSITE: In Arrowhead Trail section
   (or use Judge C.R. Magney State Park)

7.1 (2.9)
GRAVEL PIT ROAD

SHT crosses several cutover open areas with varied woods in between. Look for blueberries in open sections. For approximately 1.5 miles the SHT follows the straight borderline of private property, past Lake views and mature pines. SHT crosses old road bed upon exiting another section of private land and shortly passes bearing tree and survey line, then follows Gauthier Creek.

9.1 (0.9)
JUNCTION WITH STATE PARK TRAIL

As the trail begins to pull away from Gauthier Creek, the SHT merges with state park trail. Stay right on this grassy trail, which is a XC ski trail in the winter.

10.0 (0.0)
JUDGE C.R. MAGNEY STATE PARK TRAILHEAD

SHT enters parking lot located just north of state park campground.

Magney State Park to Arrowhead Trail

START (END)
Judge C.R. Magney State Park

SYNOPSIS
A one mile trail along the east side of the Brule River affords hikers views of Lower Falls, Upper Falls, and the Devil's Kettle. SHT continues about one mile further up the river, then dead-ends at the boundary of private property. Hikers following the SHT along the east side of the river must return to the Magney state park parking area using the same route. This section of the SHT is planned for further construction.

JUDGE C.R. MAGNEY STATE PARK

Judge C.R. Magney State Park is named after the former Minnesota Supreme Court Justice Clarence R. Magney. A strong advocate of Minnesota state parks, he was instrumental in establishing eleven parks and waysides along the North Shore. This park was established in 1957 to preserve three waterfalls on the Brule River: the Lower Falls, the Upper Falls, and the Devil's Kettle. The Devil's Kettle was named appropriately. A large rock juts out and splits the river in two. The east branch drops 50 feet to a deep gorge and pool. The west branch plunges into a huge pothole and, according to legend, disappears forever. 4514 acres in size, today the park remains relatively undeveloped with six miles of hiking trails, 36 rustic campsites, and one backpack site.

Trail Corridor to be Determined

JUDGE C.R. MAGNEY
STATE PARK

Arrowhead Trail to Jackson Lake Road

START (END)
Cook Co. Rd. 16 (Arrowhead Trail) north of Hovland

END (START)
Jackson Lake Rd.

LENGTH OF TRAIL SECTION
5.1 miles

SAFETY CONCERNS
• Blowdowns in spruce-fir forests may obscure the trail

ACCESS AND PARKING
WEST END
Nearest Hwy. 61 milepost: 128.9

Secondary road name and number: Cook Co. Rd. 16 (Arrowhead Trail)

Etc: Follow Arrowhead Trail 3.3 miles. Trailhead is on right. Parking area has room for 4–5 cars. Overnight okay.

ACCESS AND PARKING
EAST END
Continue on Arrowhead Trail 1.2 miles past western end trailhead, or 4.5 total miles from Hwy. 61. Turn right on Jackson Lake Rd. 3.0 miles on Jackson Lake Rd. to trailhead on right in a cedar swamp. Park on roadside. Caution: there are many logging trucks on this road, so park well off the roadway if possible.

FACILITIES
At starting trailhead: none

Designated campsites on this section of the SHT: one

SYNOPSIS
This section is home to the ghost of the woodland caribou. Moss-covered rocks and lichen-draped trees give this land a true boreal feel. Experience the variety as the SHT winds from open rocky ridges with wide views of the Lake and Isle Royale, into dark forests and quiet backwaters. One-half of this section follows an open rocky ridge, with nearly continual views.

MILE-BY-MILE DESCRIPTION

0.0 (5.1)
PULL-OFF ON ARROWHEAD TRAIL

SHT departs from right side of lot, nearly parallel to the road, descending steeply through aspen and fir to Carlson Creek. SHT crosses creek on 23-foot bridge, continues along creek through alder before climbing past some large spruce and up through an unusual older balsam fir stand.

0.6 (4.5)
SOUTHWEST END OF RIDGETOP

From the first view through some young aspens, the SHT meanders along this ridgeline for 1.5 miles. Cairns lead the way through mixed spruce, fir and aspen forest as the views keep getting better. Look for Isle Royale over 20 miles away. Before descending to creek, SHT enters private land. Watch for beaver meadow as SHT nears creek.

1.6 (3.5)
CREEK CROSSING

This is a small creek, crossed on mossy stepping stones. SHT skirts east edge of the beaver meadow, then climbs back to the ridgetop through dead and dying fir. Occasional large spruce show what this forest might have been like before logging or disease. In a grassy opening, faint trail goes down to homesteads below, then SHT returns to open rocky vistas, including a 180° overlook and a narrow ridge with seasonal views to both sides. SHT descends steeply from ridge into a valley, with nice views of beaver pond and Lake below. Another dark forest, once the habitat of the woodland caribou, before the SHT meets the unnamed creek where the water appears to caress the moss-covered boulders.

▲ WOODLAND CARIBOU POND CAMPSITE

TYPE: Regular
TENT PADS: 4
WATER: From beaver pond—treat before using
SETTING: 3.0 miles east of Arrowhead Trail
PREVIOUS CAMPSITE: West side of State Park
   (or use Judge C.R. Magney State Park)
NEXT CAMPSITE: 3.8 miles

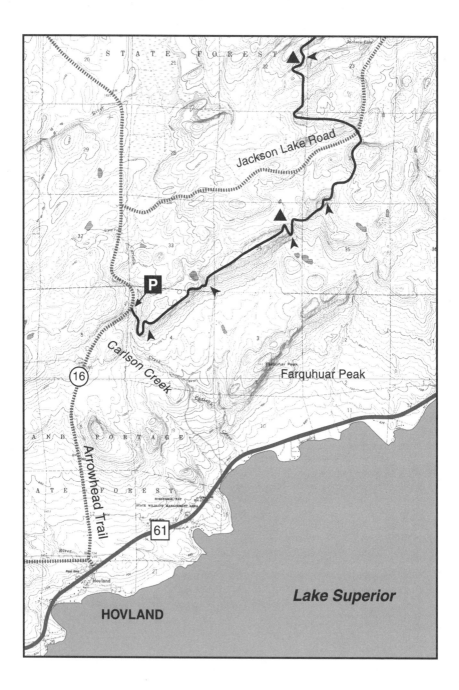

3.2 (1.9)
CREEK CROSSING

SHT crosses this well-flowing creek on a split-log footbridge, near a couple of black ash, then climbs east side of creek and, like the previous creek crossing, follows the edge of the beaver meadow. SHT climbs through a relatively mature mixed birch forest.

3.9 (1.2)
"HELLACIOUS OVERLOOK"

Steep climb rewards hikers with a wide view to Lake, Isle Royale, beaver meadows below, etc. SHT continues along ridgetop, with more views to the northeast, then descends steeply past dead and dying fir, into a wet area with alder and ash. Forest here is older and more varied than western end of section. SHT gradually climbs through aspen and birch and diseased fir, then descends steeply into a cedar swamp and across a corduroy walkway to the road.

5.1 (0.0)
JACKSON LAKE RD.

FIRE ECOLOGY

Forest fires, either by their absence or raging presence, have had significant impact on the forests of the North Shore. Fire is a natural part of many ecosystems, providing a periodic cleansing and an easy way to return nutrients to the soil. Many of the birch forests along the SHT grew up following large-scale forest fires that followed logging in the area— as evidence, look in the even-aged birch forests for the numerous large fire-charred stumps of white pines. The few remaining patches of old-growth pines have likely survived a number of fires with their thick, corky bark and out-of-reach branches. The trail's extensive maple forests, however, have thrived in part due to human suppression of fires; these northern hardwoods would not survive even a small forest fire.

Jackson Lake Road to Border Route Trail

START (END)
Jackson Lake Rd.

END (START)
Otter Lake Rd.

LENGTH OF TRAIL SECTION
8.7 miles

SAFETY CONCERNS
• The remoteness of this section makes advance planning important

ACCESS AND PARKING
WEST END
Nearest Hwy. 61 milepost: 128.9

Secondary road name and number:

Cook Co. Rd. 16 (Arrowhead Trail) to Jackson Lake Rd.

Etc: Follow Arrowhead Trail from Hwy 61, 4.5 miles to Jackson Lake Rd. Right on Jackson Lake Rd. 3.1 miles. Trailhead is on left. No official parking lot, parking is along side of road. Road is used by logging trucks so be sure car is well off road.

ACCESS AND PARKING
EAST END
Continue on Jackson Lake Rd. 5.2 miles from trailhead to Otter Lake Rd. Turn left (West) 2.0 miles to trailhead parking lot.

FACILITIES
At starting trailhead: none

Designated campsites on this section of the SHT: two

SYNOPSIS
This is the northernmost section of the trail. It connects with the Border Route Trail at the Swamp River. The SHT reaches its highest elevation, 1829 feet, on this section. Overlooks of Jackson Lake and the Upper Swamp River drainage are highlights. This is remote country, yet with significant logging influence in the northern half, it is also not wilderness.

MILE-BY-MILE DESCRIPTION

0.0 (8.7)
JACKSON LAKE ROAD
The SHT departs directly across the Jackson Lake Rd. from the
Arrowhead Trail to Jackson Lake Rd. section. The trail heads generally
westward past an active (1997) logging area to the first of several overlooks.

0.8 (7.9)
JACKSON CREEK AREA OVERLOOK
The view westward encompasses the Jackson Creek branch of the
Swamp River watershed. From here the trail heads northeastward,
staying high on the ridge. A glimpse of a small pond through the trees
signals the beginning of the descent to a small stream. Hop across the
stream on small boulders. The trail continues, trending northward
through rolling terrain to the campsite and log bridge on Jackson
Creek.

▲ JACKSON CREEK CAMPSITE

TYPE: Regular
TENT PADS: 4
WATER: From Jackson Creek
SETTING: 1.7 miles from Jackson Lake Rd.
PREVIOUS CAMPSITE: 3.8 miles
NEXT CAMPSITE: 5.3 miles

1.7 (7.0)
JACKSON CREEK BRIDGE
Jackson Creek is small but dependable. Just downstream from the
bridge is a pool approximately 3 feet deep. Cool off with a dip.
Upstream from the bridge is the site of an old beaver pond, now large-
ly drained, with a picturesque bedrock island within the pond. From
Jackson Creek the trail leads around the north end of the swampy area
before heading uphill and eastward to several partial overlooks above
Jackson Lake. Choose one as the ideal spot for a lunch stop. SHT
drops off from the Jackson Lake Ridge into a cedar forest on the valley
floor. It then climbs upward to several bedrock outcroppings on the
eastern face of the SHT's highest hill. Before reaching the high point,

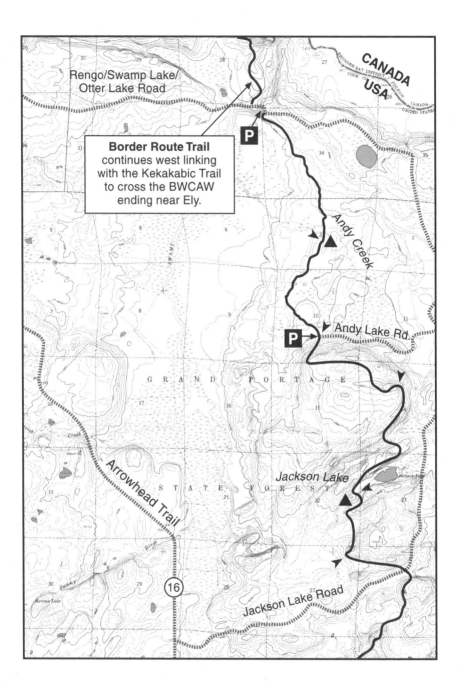

Border Route Trail continues west linking with the Kekakabic Trail to cross the BWCAW ending near Ely.

Rengo/Swamp Lake/ Otter Lake Road

CANADA

USA

Andy Creek

Andy Lake Rd.

GRAND PORTAGE

Arrowhead Trail

STATE FOREST

Jackson Lake

(16)

Jackson Lake Road

the Trail drops onto the north slope of the hill, then climbs steeply to the summit plateau.

3.8 (4.9)
HIGHEST POINT OF TRAIL
The high point, 1,829 feet, is in the midst of a mixed forest. There is no view. Continuing west along the summit plateau, views northward can be glimpsed through the trees. Raspberries grow profusely in this area. (The name Rosebush Ridge appears on some maps—apparently because the explorer was torn apart by thorns and in his/her pain did not properly identify the culprit species.) The SHT drops steeply northward to the Andy Lake Rd.

5.3 (3.4)
ANDY LAKE ROAD
The final section of trail from Andy Lake Rd., an active logging road, to the Otter Lake/Rengo Rd. is predominantly flat. It passes through recent logged-over areas as well as open meadows of older logged areas. Midway is Andy Creek and its campsite.

▲ ANDY CREEK CAMPSITE

TYPE: Regular
TENT PADS: 4
WATER: From Andy Creek
SETTING: 1.7 miles south of Otter Lake Rd.
PREVIOUS CAMPSITE: 5.3 miles
NEXT CAMPSITE: 1.7 miles (USFS campsite at Swamp River);
   permit required

7.0 (1.7)
ANDY CREEK BRIDGE
The SHT may be hard to follow if not recently weed whipped in the meadow areas. If so, continue north and slightly west. Follow what were obviously old logging roads to the Otter Lake Rd. This is the northern terminus of the SHT. The Swamp River is about 300 feet westward along the road.

8.7 (0.0)
CAMPSITE AT THE SWAMP RIVER
This site is actually a public access to the Swamp River. There may be vehicles parked here or fishermen coming and going with motor boats. Tents can be set up anywhere in the parking area. A latrine, waste bucket, and fire ring are present.

A short side trip on the Border Route Trail is recommended. One mile northward on the BRT from the Swamp River Campsite is a wonderful overlook. Below lies the confluence of the Swamp and Pigeon Rivers. Northward is a view encompassing miles of Canadian wilderness. Southward is a great view of the broad Swamp River Valley. Eastward hills march into the distance. Somewhere out there lies Lake Superior.

More About the Border Route Trail
The Border Route Trail, like the SHT, is a trail dependent on volunteers. The Minnesota Rovers Outing Club began building the trail in 1972. By 1981 they had completed over 75 miles of trail construction, linking the Gunflint Lake area in the west and the Grand Portage Trail in the east.

The trail follows the Canadian border, usually high on ridges overlooking lakes and streams as much as 500 feet below. The majority of the trail is within the BWCAW. Federal rules and regulations apply. Permits are required for hiking in the BWCAW. From where the SHT meets the Border Route at the Swamp River, the BRT heads west for 65.4 miles to the Gunflint Trail and the nearby eastern trailhead of the Kekekabic Trail. The "Kek" slices through the heart of the BWCAW for 40 miles terminating near Snowbank Lake on the Fernberg Rd. outside of Ely.

Future plans (as of 2001) call for the union of the Kekekabic, Border Route, and Superior Hiking Trails under the banner of the North Country Trail. The NCT is a National Scenic Trail extending from North Dakota to Vermont. In Minnesota, the route would connect Tamarack National Wildlife Refuge, Itasca State Park, the Chippewa

National Forest, the new Mesabi Range Trail, the Kekekabic, Border Route, and Superior Hiking Trails, Duluth, and Jay Cooke State Park.

The Border Route Trail continues east from the Swamp River, SHT trailhead for 7 miles. This section is seldom used and as of this writing very obscure. The first 1.8 miles use the Otter Lake Rd. The trail then heads down to the Pigeon River which it follows to Fort Charlotte and the western end of the Grand Portage Trail which, in turn, leads 9 miles to Lake Superior.

The Border Route Trail can be used in conjunction with the SHT for some truly wild hiking experiences. In general, the Border Route is more rugged and less well maintained. Expect to use your maps, guidebook and compass.

The guidebook *The Border Route Trail—A Trail Guide and Map,* by Marcia Scott and Chuck Hoffman, is available from the SHT store or direct from the Minnesota Rovers Outing Club, P. O. Box 14133, Dinkytown Station, Minneapolis, MN 55414

The Kekekabic Trail guidebook, *The Hiker's BWCA Wilderness Companion: Kekekabic Trail Guide,* by Martin Kubic and Angela Anderson, is also available from the SHT store or direct from the Kekekabic Trail Club, c/o Midwest Mountaineering, 309 Cedar Ave., Minneapolis, MN 55454.

Towns Along the Superior Hiking Trail

The communities listed are those accessible from the Superior Hiking Trail.

COMMUNITY	ZIP	SERVICES	MEDICAL	HWY. 61 MILEPOST
Two Harbors	55616	M, L, G, C, LM, O	Hospital	26.1
Castle Danger	No PO	M, LG, L	—	37.1
Beaver Bay	55601	M, L, LG, LM	—	51.0
Silver Bay	55614	M, L, G, LM	Clinic	54.3
Illgen City	No PO	L	—	59.3
Finland	55603	M, L, G	—	59.3
Schroeder	55613	M, L, LG, C	—	79.0
Tofte	55615	M, L, G, O	—	82.6
Lutsen	55612	M, L, G	—	91.7
Grand Marais	55604	M, L, G, C, LM, O	Hospital	109.5

SERVICES
M = meals
L = lodging
G = groceries
LG = limited groceries
C = camping
LM = laundromat
O = outfitting supplies

EMERGENCIES
911 in all three counties

MAIL
Hiker's mail should be marked "General Delivery—Hold for hiker on Superior Hiking Trail." Post office hours vary.

ADDITIONAL INFORMATION
• Superior Hiking Trail Association
PO Box 4, 731 Seventh Ave. (Hwy 61), Two Harbors, MN 55616
tel (218) 834-2700, fax (218) 834-4436, e-mail suphike@mr.net
www.shta.org

• H.T. Leasing LTD. (Bus service)
Happy Time Tours, 1480 West Walsh St., Thunder Bay, Ontario, Canada, P7E 6H6 (807) 473-5955

• Lodge to Lodge Hiking Program: Boundary Country Trekking (800) 322-8327 or (218) 388-9972

• Lutsen-Tofte Tourism Association
P.O. Box 2248, Tofte, MN 55615 (218) 663-7804

• Minnesota State Parks: DNR Parks, 500 Lafayette Rd., St. Paul, MN 55155 (800) 652-9747 or (612) 296-6157
For reservations at state park campgrounds:
(800) 246-2267 or (612) 922-9000

• R.J. Houle Visitor Information Center for Lake County
8 Hwy. 61 East, Two Harbors, MN 55616
(800) 554-2116 or (218) 834-4005

• Superior Shuttle, Dan Sanders
960 Hwy. 61 East, Two Harbors, MN 55616 (218) 834-5511

• Tip of the Arrowhead Association
Grand Marais, MN 55604 (800) 622-4014

• U.S.D.A. Forest Service:
Tofte Ranger Station (218) 663-7280
Grand Marais Ranger Station (Gunflint Ranger District)
(218) 387-1750

A Final Note

The trouble is, we're tempted to think that a guided description can really describe and guide. Of course, no matter how well done, it cannot. It depends on what we're looking for.

The Superior Hiking Trail leads us from the mountain tops to the valley floors, to the deep woods and the cascading rivers. A guide can describe a rocky overlook at such and so, but it cannot tell whether it's fogged in or not.

And who's to say whether we find in the fog the mystery of the north woods, or whether we find disappointment in not seeing farther?

I'd like to pick a defining experience, a place and time on the Trail where it all came together for me in some kind of mystical peak experience. The retelling of this, I believe, could show the true value of the Trail. But would it really? We can wax poetically all we want about the North Shore and the ridgeline, and it will all be true. The truth is, the value we experience depends on what we're seeking.

Instead, for me, faces come to mind. It is the faces and personalities of all those who brought the Trail to life with sweat and good humor. It is Mark, Duane, Bob, Cory, Toivo, Neil, Harry, Stormy, and forty others who did the actual work of trail building. It is John, Tom, Bill, and Anne who, by the force of their character, willed the Trail into existence.

For this trail to be really worthwhile, it should be more than just fun. It should heighten our awareness and appreciation of all that is natural. It should make us realize our place in the diverse complex web that is the land. With a little luck and a little help it might, for a few of us. And that would be worthwhile.

— TOM PETERSON

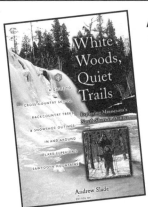

AND WHEN YOU NEED THE ULTIMATE GUIDEBOOK FOR ENJOYING WINTER ON THE NORTH SHORE...

The North Shore is one of the most beautiful regions on earth, and home to some of the best cross-country skiing in North America. It's a place where you can snowshoe through deep woods to stunning overlooks, and where you can thrill to signs of wolf, moose and raven. Here, perfectly groomed ski trails have earned names like Bear Chase, Otter Run, Mystery Mountain, Canyon Curves, Magnetic Rock and Lonely Lake. Now you can easily find winter trails in this user-friendly, comprehensive guide which covers the region from Duluth-Superior north to Thunder Bay. Let *White Woods, Quiet Trails* guide you to:

• 900 kilometers of groomed cross-country ski trails including detailed maps and trail descriptions.

• Snowshoeing routes on more than 200 miles of the SHT, in seven Minnesota State Parks and in quiet places throughout the region.

• Exploration of frozen North Shore rivers, including river access points and level of difficulty.

• The sights and sounds of a North Shore winter landscape and its wildlife.

• Enjoying winter activities safely.

For winter fun, you'll want to open these pages and hit the trail!

**WHITE WOODS, QUIET TRAILS:
EXPLORING MINNESOTA'S NORTH SHORE IN WINTER**
A guide to cross-country skiing, backcountry treks & snowshoe outings in and around Lake Superior's Sawtooth Mountains **$15.95**

Available from the Superior Hiking Trail Association
(218) 834-2700 or from your favorite bookstore.

Join the Superior Hiking Trail Association!

APPLICATION FOR MEMBERSHIP OR RENEWAL
(Note: Memberships run for one year from receipt of application)

Membership Categories:
(Check type of membership desired)

❏ Student . . . .$15   ❏ Individual $25
❏ Family 35   ❏ Youth organization/
❏ Supporting 100   Non-profit 40
❏ Life Member 500   ❏ Donation$_____

BUSINESS/CORPORATE

❏ Contributing . . . . . .$100   ❏ Sustaining $500
❏ Supporting 250   ❏ Patron 1,000
❏ Donation $_____

Enclosed is $ _____ for (check below):
❏ **New membership**
❏ **Renewal   (Member number_____)**

Name: _____

Address: _____

_____

Home Tel: _____   Work Tel: _____

The Superior Hiking Trail Association is composed of volunteers.
To accomplish our goals, we need the active involvement of our members.

I am interested in helping the Superior Hiking Trail Association through:

❏ Constructing trails   ❏ Maintaining trails
❏ Fund-raising   ❏ Promotion/Publicity/Marketing
❏ Programs (leading hikes)   ❏ Art/Photography
❏ Group presentations
❏ Special skills: _____
❏ Liaison with other organizations
    (name of group) _____

MAIL TO Superior Hiking Trail Assn., PO Box 4, Two Harbors, MN 55616